The LITTLE BLACK BOOK *of* STRATEGIC PLANNING
FOR DISTRIBUTORS

Brent R. Grover

Published by:
Gale Media Inc.
303-443-5060
www.mdm.com

Gale Media Inc. is the publisher of Modern Distribution Management and mdm.com, and owner of Industrial Market Information.

Edited by Lindsay Konzak and Jenel Stelton-Holtmeier
Cover and Interior Design by Dillon Calkins and Todd Mitchell
Modern Distribution Management

ISBN 978-0615655017

CONTENTS

Introduction

We had a small sign in the lobby of our distribution business. It was one of those black signs with moveable white type so the inspirational messages could be changed every so often, like those in front of old churches in small towns. The messages were supposed to help motivate the staff. I've forgotten most of them, but one of the corny sayings I do remember was: "If you don't know where you're going, any road will take you there."

Planning is not one of the things that most distributors do best. The National Association of Wholesaler-Distributors' first-ever *Facing the Forces of Change* reported that in 1982 only 4% of distribution companies in the survey did strategic planning. That minute percentage paled in comparison to the more than 50% of suppliers in the study who stated that their firms had strategic plans. Almost 30 years later, in a more recent survey with *Modern Distribution Management* readers, we found similar though not as stark difference between distributors and suppliers, with almost 60% of suppliers and 40% of distributors reporting using a formal planning process.

Is the underuse of planning by distributors a result of the companies being smaller? That is clearly one of the factors, since larger companies are more likely to take planning very seriously. Another underlying cause is that so many of the firms are privately owned by families whose leaders tend to keep too many things to themselves. There is also a perception among distributors that planning strategy is not as important for them as it is for manufacturing businesses that are more complex and need to commit large amounts of capital to equipment or for organizations that are growing rapidly such as technology businesses.

My first encounter with strategic planning as a practitioner was in the early '80s when 3M, a major supplier to our packaging distribution company, hosted a three-day workshop conducted by my former employer Arthur Andersen & Co. Each distribution company team in the class was challenged to draft a strategic plan for their businesses. Andersen's methodology was "classic" strategic planning. We did a SWOT analysis (strengths, weaknesses, opportunities, threats) followed by an internal and external environment scan. As basic as the Andersen process was, our management priorities went through a metamorphosis. We committed ourselves to setting goals, using key indicators and speeding up the change process. We boldly moved into new business areas and decisively moved out of others. Strategic planning made an immediate, lasting and positive difference.

This simple but effective process contrasts with other approaches I've seen through the years.

Notable management schools at universities in large cities proffer executive training programs to an audience of managers from local companies, generally seminars about a specific management topic. In the early '90s I attended a series of eight Saturday morning classes at Case Western Reserve advertised as "managing a fast-growing business" or something similar. My expectations were high. Earlier in my career I had taught all but two of the accounting department courses at Case. It turned out that my expectations outstripped what was delivered. The instructors were volunteers, big-company executives and consultants from huge firms, not members of the university faculty. The only thing Case seemed to actually have to do with the program was providing some classrooms not otherwise used on Saturdays.

The major corporations and big-time consultants had planning specialists who apparently spent all of their time studying reports and participating in large meetings. The company people did not seem to know much about how their companies transacted business with customers and suppliers, how they won and lost against competitors, and what the people in their company actually did. The consultants were mostly entry-level staff with stunning academic credentials but no actual business experience. We learned about strategic planning projects that spanned many months and required numerous meetings with large numbers of managers. The deliverable, as they say, was a set of heavy binders filled with documentation such as meeting minutes, memoranda and charts. The Corporate America approach to planning strategy appeared to better meet the needs of the planners than those they were planning for.

I learned that distribution firms needed to plan, but not this way.

The TEC group I belonged to for five years in the late '90s was the best source of strategic planning advice I got while I was a distributor CEO. TEC (now Vistage) groups consist of a dozen or so CEOs, usually from medium-sized companies, who meet monthly as a group with a facilitator. Most of the meetings include several hours with a professional trainer whose job is to educate people to become better CEOs. The idea of a "one-page strategic plan" percolated up from the TEC speakers. We learned the value of creating a summary of the company's plan in a form that can be used to inculcate the plan in the minds of employees, to get them excited about where the business is going and to clarify their roles in it. Data to back up the plan's assumptions and conclusions needed to exist, but were not presented in the plan itself. I learned the value of planning insights from seasoned, knowledgeable, independent outsiders from my TEC group.

I started working with distributors outside our company about 20 years ago by serving on the boards of two businesses, a larger ($125 million in sales) distributor of X-ray supplies and equipment and a similarly sized distributor of motion control products. As an outside board member it was easier for me to see what was happening at these businesses and what was likely coming around the corner than it was for the people who ran the companies on a daily basis. How would the digital photography revolution change the X-ray film industry? How would rapid consolidation affect the traditional branding and exclusive distribution policies of industrial equipment suppliers?

We sold our distribution businesses in 1999. After completing my contractual obligations to the private equity firm that bought us, I wanted to stay active in the distribution industry. So I started Evergreen Consulting, LLC just after 9/11, an auspicious time to try something new. Consulting, speaking and writing was a good recipe for an experienced CEO who also happened to be a former college instructor and a recovering accountant (old CPAs never lose their green eyeshades). Naturally I had a strategic plan for Evergreen Consulting. The focus would be the wholesale distribution channel in North America. The projects would be about profitable growth: strategic plan facilitation, advising about acquisitions to jumpstart growth, and strategic pricing. I decided to concentrate on long-term relationships with a handful of key clients until finding the right partner or partners enabled expansion of the practice. Evergreen Consulting would bring together what I learned and experienced as a distributor CEO, CPA, college instructor, board member and TEC member.

Over the past 10 years our team has facilitated strategic planning assignments for U.S. and Canadian wholesale distributors ranging in revenue size from $30 million to $300 million and in many trade lines. In this book, I share what we have learned, including the pitfalls alongside what works.

I share planning tips and tools developed over years of facilitating many planning engagements with leading distributors. How many and who should be on your planning team? How many meetings should you have? What should be on the meeting agendas? How long should the process take? How can you increase the chances of success? What's the best way to monitor execution results? How often is strategic planning necessary? Is an outside facilitator really needed?

The insights in *The Little Black Book of Strategic Planning* will help you and your facilitator organize a strategic planning project, gather the needed information and build your one-page strategic plan. You will also find practical advice about implementing the plan. Execution is the final step, and it is where many distributors fail. You will need a system to monitor results and take corrective action. This book includes what you will need to put your plan into action – a plan specifically tuned for a wholesale distribution company.

By trial and error, both inside our paper and packaging and janitorial supplies businesses, as well as at the distribution companies where I served as a board member, I found that strategic planning for distributors must be simple enough to be easily understood but not so simple as to overlook anything important. The project must include operating managers but not so many that the process becomes bogged down. There must be several meetings but not so many that the process becomes a burden. An outside facilitator is needed but not one who has too little experience, who does not understand distribution or who is unaffordable. The project cannot take so long that people lose interest, but it must not be so rushed that all reasonable options are not considered and that significant risks are not weighed.

This concise book frames all the above parameters to help you get the best result from strategic planning – one that fits your company's needs and culture.

Your job as an owner, CEO or senior executive is to make your company better every year and to build shareholder value. This book can help you get there.

Brent R. Grover

Chapter 1

The Strategic Planning Horizon & One-Page Plan

I was introduced to the idea of formal strategic planning in the 1970s by the accounting firm Arthur Andersen & Co., my former employer. The firm was a great innovator of business ideas for their clients in the wholesale distribution industry. It took a special interest in our industry and positioned its executives as leaders through its association with the National Association of Wholesaler-Distributors. Andersen was the originator of the NAW's widely known *Facing the Forces of Change* series, first published in 1982. One of the findings in that inaugural study was that only 4% of wholesale distributors engaged in formal strategic planning, while over half of the industry's suppliers did so[1].

In a more recent survey of readers of *Modern Distribution Management* completed in late 2011, we found similar differences between distributors and suppliers. Almost 60% of suppliers reported using a formal planning process with one-third using an informal process. Only about 10% have no planning process. By contrast, 40% of distributors in the survey use a formal process, but a larger group – about half – use an informal process.

The idea of strategic planning for corporations evolved in the 1960s from military planning concepts, starting with the distinction between "strategy" and "tactics." Followers of military thinkers such as Von Clausewitz (*On War*) and Sun-Tzu (*The Art of War*) learn about military maneuvers like flanking attacks and frontal attacks. A comparison can

---

1 See *Facing the Forces of Change* by Arthur Andersen & Co. for the Distribution Research & Education Foundation (DREF). Published by National Association of Wholesaler-Distributors, 1982.

Figure 1-1: Strategic Planning Among Distributors & Manufacturers

In a 2011 survey of Modern Distribution Management readers, more manufacturers than distributors had a formal planning process in place.

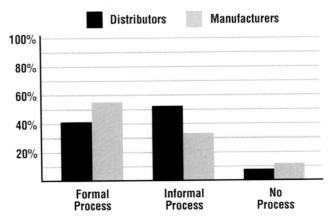

be made between business and war. Some business leaders see themselves as Samurai and the competitors as enemies, but not everyone thinks that way.

Perhaps the generation of business leaders who fought World War II were more receptive to Michael Porter's *Competitive Strategy* when it appeared in 1965. This Harvard professor-cum-consultant was the catalyst for a wave of corporate interest in strategy. Big-time consulting firms Boston Consulting and McKinsey, among others, became the go-to experts for major corporations embarking on strategic planning projects. Larger companies appointed directors of planning and created planning departments. This explains why the suppliers – many being large firms – were so far ahead of distributors in planning when the 1982 NAW survey was done.

The strategic planning process can be described as a series of layers, as shown by Verne Harnish in a pyramid[2] , which inspired the Distributor

---

2 See *Mastering the Rockefeller Habits: What You Must Do to Increase the Value of Your Growing Firm*, by Verne Harnish. Published by SelectBooks Inc., 2002.

Chapter 1 - The Strategic Planning Horizon & One-Page Plan

Figure 1-2: Distributor Planning Pyramid

Daily task list

Quarterly, monthly, weekly

Annual business plan

Three-year planning horizon

Leader's vision and expectations

Unchanging bedrock values

Planning Pyramid in Figure 1-2.

The time horizon shown on the pyramid is three years, but any choice of planning horizon is a compromise: Too short doesn't carry you far enough into the future, too long is farther than we can see. I recommend distributors conduct a thorough strategic planning exercise every third year, and that the business plans for the intervening years be tied into the strategic plan. That planning cycle has withstood the test of time.

An obvious objection to a three-year horizon is that our world is changing so fast that the plan will become obsolete. Indeed, all plans become obsolete the day they are completed. They may be obsolete before they are complete. No battle plan survives contact with the enemy, and no business plan is intact after engagement with the marketplace. A business needs to adapt to incoming information about changes on the playing field, to competitors' moves, and to unforeseeable customer and oves. Plan, and adjust when needed.

The Process

Think of strategic planning as a story, and like all good stories, it has a beginning, a middle and an end. The strategic planning story includes characters, a plot, some mystery and possibly even a hero or two.

The story begins with the leader's vision for the company, the second layer of the planning pyramid. This sits on top of a foundation, the company's values, which do not change over time. The leader plays

Figure 1-3: Strategic Planning Process Flow Diagram

This flow diagram breaks the distributor strategic planning process into four bite-size pieces. Each piece, made up of three or four parts, is completed in sequence. Planning team members need to know how the process is going to unfold and where the team is at any given time. The group may become impatient and want to go directly to the breakthrough initiatives. That would be a mistake! The groundwork must be laid carefully to build support and to be sure that all reasonable possibilities are considered but that the company's constraints are kept in perspective.

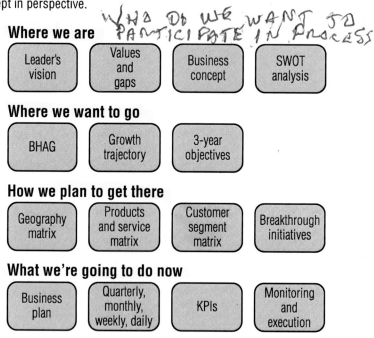

WHO DO WE WANT TO PARTICIPATE IN PROCESS

Where we are

- Leader's vision
- Values and gaps
- Business concept
- SWOT analysis

Where we want to go

- BHAG
- Growth trajectory
- 3-year objectives

How we plan to get there

- Geography matrix
- Products and service matrix
- Customer segment matrix
- Breakthrough initiatives

What we're going to do now

- Business plan
- Quarterly, monthly, weekly, daily
- KPIs
- Monitoring and execution

Chapter 1 - The Strategic Planning Horizon & One-Page Plan

the role of the progenitor in this section, describing what inspires him and sharing insight about the industry as well as perception about what the business needs to be in the future. The hour or so spent discussing the leader's vision is vital to the work that follows, as the company's plan must be in synch with that vision. This section is also a test of the leader's creativity, intuition and taste for innovation.

Next is a review of the status quo. Homeostasis refers to the tendency of an organism (or an organization) to seek equilibrium between inter-dependent forces. Once this delicate balance is obtained, the firm tends to resist changes that interfere with the equilibrium. Discussion of the existing state of affairs starts with the company's values and gaps. This part of planning involves a group discussion of the organization's values and discovery of where the company doesn't "walk the talk." The larger the gaps, the more important it is to rectify them before trying to make changes.

Planning Tip

Pass out blank copies of the One-Page Plan at the first meeting of the strategic planning team. Show the group a completed plan for a hypothetical company so they can understand what a solid plan includes.

Next comes the assessment of the status quo. The assessment is gathered through interviews and surveys, and results are published in a briefing book. Breakout groups do a SWOT exercise as part of this discussion. The SWOT activity – examining the company's strengths, weaknesses, opportunities and threats – highlights and prioritizes the company's enablers and constraints.

We examine the company's playing field: What has happened since the last planning exercise? What have competitors done? What has the company done? What could happen that might devastate the company? This portion can be streamlined by compiling answers to these questions in briefing reports from the company's business unit managers. In smaller companies, the planning team members may be the business unit managers, and the discussion is more spontaneous.

Moving on, we determine the driving force of the business, the source of the company's profit. The company's strategy must be based on this driving force.

We hash out a business concept and follow that up with an elevator speech based on that concept.

A Compelling Goal, Growth Trajectory, Three-Year Objectives and Key Performance Indicators (KPIs) mark the beginning of formal strategy formulation, starting with what business author Jim Collins terms your Big Hairy Audacious Goal, or BHAG[3]. This section includes a "confrontation of the brutal facts,"[4] including a discussion of the company's financial statements, cash flow, operating cycle and strategic profit model.[5]

Next up: a strategic value map and the sandboxes (customer segments, products and services, and geographic markets). The strategic value map is based on a detailed analysis of the business prepared in advance but not revealed until this point in the process. The three sandboxes are at the heart of implementing the company's strategy.

The planning team fleshes out and prioritizes breakthrough initiatives. An outside facilitator leading this part is critical. The team needs to maintain focus, stay in thinking mode and think broadly but without wasting time.

The team is now ready to finalize the One-Page Plan and move into the

---

3 See *Built to Last: Successful Habits of Visionary Companies*, by Jim Collins and Jerry I. Porras. Published by HarperBusiness, 1995.

4 See *Good to Great: Why Some Companies Make the Leap ... and Others Don't*, Jim Collins. Published by HarperBusiness, 2001.

5 See my *Official Guide to Wholesaler-Distributor Financial Success*. Published by National Association of Wholesaler-Distributors, 2007. Go to www.nawpubs.org for ordering information.

Chapter 1 - The Strategic Planning Horizon & One-Page Plan

execution and monitoring phase of the planning project.

I outline each of these steps in detail in this book. Take it one chapter at a time, or use this book as a guide for your next strategic planning retreat. Throughout the book, I also provide Planning Tips to help you adapt the book's material in a planning retreat setting.

The One-Page Plan

Verne Harnish first came up with the One-Page Strategic Plan.[6] The idea of a One-Page Plan struck me as odd when I first considered it. The usual image of a strategic plan is a huge document, maybe a set of three-ring binders, with hundreds of pages of text and graphs. It's also well-known that many companies have spent huge amounts of time and money writing the perfect (or nearly perfect) plan only to show a presentation to the board of directors and then place the binders in the corporate archives.

But musty books on a dusty shelf don't do anything to address the imperatives of a compelling goal, role clarity and mutual trust. The CEO and other leaders need to tell the troops, in their own words:

1. This is where we're going.
2. This is why we're going there.
3. This is how we're going to get there.
4. This is when we expect to arrive.
5. This is how we'll know where we are.
6. This is your role in getting us there.
7. This is what you'll get when we arrive.

I adapted the One-Page Plan idea for wholesale distributors. The distributor one-pager makes most of the answers to the seven questions accessible to those who need to know and understand: the people who make it happen. The company's plan is not just the plan for the board,

---

6 See *Mastering the Rockefeller Habits: What You Must Do to Increase the Value of Your Growing Firm*, by Verne Harnish. Published by SelectBooks Inc., 2002.

for the C-level executives, or for the managers and supervisors. It is the company's plan, which means it is everyone's plan.

Like all good ideas, there may be drawbacks to sharing the plan with everyone in the organization. For example, the plan may leak out from indiscreet employees. Suppliers, customers and competitors may get the information. The one-pager needs to be scrubbed so that information that could harm the company does not appear on the document that everyone sees. The plan can be shared at meetings on the screen but not printed out and distributed.

Not all companies believe in open-book management or feel that employees need to understand the financial objectives in the plan. The objectives can be simplified to overcome this objection; however I suggest that employee education[7] on financial objectives begin now so that the people can share in and benefit from Key Performance Indicators (KPIs) for their own functional areas, as well as for the entire company.

Use the One-Page Plan on the following page or use the copy provided on the CD that accompanies this book. You can also access all handouts and graphics in this book at www.strategicplanningfordistributors.com with the password: handouts.

Throughout this book, we will indicate items that you can include on your One-Page Plan with this icon.

---

[7] See my *Official Guide to Wholesaler-Distributor Financial Success.* Published by National Association of Wholesaler-Distributors, 2007.

ONE-PAGE STRATEGIC PLAN

BIG HAIRY AUDACIOUS GOAL (BHAG):

ONE SENTENCE DESCRIPTION OF BUSINESS CONCEPT: _____

GEOGRAPHIC AREAS	GROW	MAINTAIN	HARVEST

PRODUCTS & SERVICES	GROW	MAINTAIN	HARVEST

CUSTOMER SEGMENTS	GROW	MAINTAIN	HARVEST

OBJECTIVES FOR THREE YEARS FROM NOW:

SALES: $ _____

GROSS MARGIN: _____ %

PRETAX PROFIT: $ _____

PERSONNEL PRODUCTIVITY RATIO: _____ %

DEBT RATIO: _____ %

DAYS SALES OUTSTANDING: _____

INVENTORY TURNS: _____

BREAKTHROUGH BUSINESS STRATEGIES TO SUPPORT THE BHAG AND OBJECTIVES:

1.

2.

✓ STRATEGY CHECKPOINT

Use these questions to help you think about strategic planning for your distribution business. Consider your own answers for these questions, and pose them to your management team. These questions are great fodder for starting the conversation on strategy.

1. If you tried strategic planning in the past, what did you like and not like about the process? Looking back, how do you feel about the plan? How well did the management team execute the plan?

2. If you haven't previously used a formal strategic planning process, what are some of the reasons you decided not to? How might the business have benefited if you had had a strategic plan in place for the past three years?

3. When your management team meets, how much time do you spend discussing the future of the business as opposed to day-to-day problems?

Chapter 2

Getting Started

Before you get started, take stock of your own vision for the business. Focus on what you want to accomplish during the remainder of your time at the company. Every CEO (including owner-CEOs) wants to leave behind a legacy of his time at the helm of the enterprise.

For some people that legacy is to reach a specific goal. Think about people who feel an urge to climb Mount Everest, break 80 on the golf course or run a marathon. In distribution business terms, that may be reaching a sales level or becoming the largest distributor of a leading manufacturer's product line.

It may be a deeply personal quest, something that makes sense only to that individual. In family businesses the personal goal may be reaching a level of success that the previous generation had only dreamed of. Founders may have goals from before they started their businesses, such as becoming financially independent and able to make a large charitable bequest to validate the sacrifices they made during their careers. Professional managers may be motivated to prove their competence, especially if they were passed over for a leadership position they coveted many years ago.

The CEO's goal is sometimes more concrete, such as seeing their hand-picked successor take over the business and build it out further. Jim Collins described CEOs who are determined to position their companies for future success as Level 5 Leaders.[1] A variation of this theme is the

---

1 See *Good to Great: Why Some Companies Make the Leap … and Others Don't,* by Jim Collins. Published by HarperBusiness, 2001.

leader who wants to provide a wonderful business opportunity for the next generation of his family. The most specific goals are often monetary: The CEO who wants to exit the business with a large amount of personal wealth, and to do so at a young enough age to start another business or just enjoy a fabulous retirement.

Business leaders, especially owners of private companies, are sometimes reluctant to confront their goals. The root causes may be feelings of guilt, embarrassment or even a sense of betrayal to their subordinates. In our work with family-owned distributors, we talk with leaders who are conflicted between their desires to leave a family legacy to their heirs and the urge to sell their companies. We see the tension as a reflection of the amount of confidence the current ownership has in the ability of the next generation to manage the company, as well as get along with each other. Complicating factors may be the need for liquidity and problems dividing family assets among working and non-working members of the succeeding generation. In some cases, selling the business is the simplest solution.

Privately owned distribution businesses, whether led by a family member or not, depend heavily on managers and other employees who are critical to past and future success. These individuals typically do not have direct ownership of the company's stock. They may not see a sale of the business by the family as being in their best interests. The leader and other owners may have a difficult time sorting out their long-term goals for the company, and they may be afraid to share their feelings with others.

The privately owned distribution business whose leader is not an owner is in a special situation. The interests of this individual and the ownership must be well-aligned. We would argue that this person must have equity or phantom equity[2] that connects his future with that of the owners.

---

[2] Phantom stock and other forms of quasi-equity are deferred compensation techniques based on future changes in the value of the business. A major ownership change usually triggers the payment of deferred compensation.

As a leader you don't necessarily need to reveal your innermost secrets to your staff. You simply need to understand what you want to achieve with your business so that a facilitator can help you guide the organization in the right direction at the right pace.

The facilitator will help the CEO determine how much risk is acceptable. Many times the leader's goals for the business aren't possible without borrowing a great deal of money, personally guaranteeing bank debt, diluting ownership by finding investors or possibly investing personal capital in the business. Sometimes the need for growth capital may require the owner to take less money out of the business. In any event, growth plans may outstrip the resources of the capital and cash flow of the business.

The leader also has to face the brutal fact that there are obstacles to growth for the company. The barriers may include lack of support of key vendors, inadequate size of the company's geographic markets, inability

Figure 2-1: Enablers and Constraints to Growth

It can be difficult to convince distributors to be honest with themselves about problems such as those in the table below: overdependence on generous vendor terms, heavy concentration on one or two major suppliers or customers, inefficient processes and staff and so on. The planning team must accept that some problems must be resolved before embarking on new initiatives and that sometimes strategic options are limited by serious shortcomings.

Enablers	Constraints
Credit support	Limited capital
Relationships with suppliers	Supplier concentration
Relationships with large accounts	Customer concentration
Customer service commitment	Inefficient back-office operations
Excellent reputation with customers	Lack of scale
Experienced business developers	Not enough business development time

to attract enough capable workers, intense competition or perhaps inadequate demand for the company's products and services.

At this stage, this is strictly a private discussion between the leader and the facilitator. The CEO's perception of the future of the company must be balanced with reality.

Values and Gaps

No plan, no matter how well-designed, can be carried out successfully if there are large gaps between the company's values and reality. Most distributors have stated values that appear in mission statements, such as the importance of quality, commitment to customers and employees, and the desire to give back to the community. That is all good stuff, but it's fairly universal and hard to measure.

For planning purposes, the team needs to look closely at what the company's leaders say about what the company stands for. These values

Figure 2-2: Getting to the Bottom of Gaps

Distributors often tout that their companies are great places to work, or that they are easy for customers to do business with. They sometimes don't have the data to back up those claims. Even worse, the facts may contradict the boasting. When gaps between stated values and the facts are found, management must fill the gaps before trying to change the company's strategy. A root cause analysis may uncover problems with company culture, business processes, training or management itself.

Value	Gap	Root Causes
Great company to work for	High turnover of top performers	Poor supervision, lack of accountability, bad working conditions
Loyal customers	Low retention rate of profitable customers	Indifferent customer service, high costs, processes out of control
Quality products	High return rate and low reorder rates	Badly designed products, inferior materials, processes out of control

are usually considered to be unchanging, nonnegotiable standards: The company is a great place to work, the company is easy to do business with, or the company stands behind its products, for example. Values are always positive things (easy to do business with) and gaps are always negative things (hard to do business with).

In many distribution companies, other members of the planning team may have strong views about the company's future, especially if those team members have committed net worth to buy shares. They should be encouraged to be honest about what's working and what's not working in the business, including the performance of the management team. Draw out individual perspectives on what is truly important to the business's future success – its values – and whether the company is living up to them.

Clearly state each value and then take it for a test drive. If one of the company's core values is that it is a great place to work, test it. Are good people leaving your company? If so, that does not support the idea that your company is a good place to work.

What is the root cause of this unhappiness? Poor working conditions, inadequate training and technology that is hard to use are among the most common. Use employee surveys to unearth these answers. Gaps are obstacles to executing a strategic plan. No matter how great the plan seems to be, the plan is worthless if it cannot be implemented. Gaps, if any, need to be filled before moving forward.

✅ STRATEGY CHECKPOINT

Use these questions to clarify your vision for your distribution business. You may want to share some of these questions with key managers to spark discussion and better communicate your thoughts on the future of the business with key decision-makers.

1. Are likely successors for the company's leadership positions currently working at the company? Have you identified them?

2. Are one or more members of the company's leadership team close to retirement?

3. If the company is privately owned, does the business have the financial strength to redeem the equity of the senior generation of owners?

4. Does the company have a strong enough capital base to make investments in significant growth?

5. If the company is controlled by a family, are there qualified and interested candidates available to potentially lead the business in the future?

6. If the company is family-controlled, is the senior generation of owners willing to take the risks needed to build the business and pass it along to the next generation?

Chapter 3
Assessment of the Status Quo

Planning is the "art of the possible" as opposed to the idea of blue sky. Distributors have precious little time to devote to planning, and because every minute counts, dreaming about things that cannot happen may be fun, but is a waste of time.

Assessment is a tightly organized process of gathering information needed to understand what the company's enablers and constraints are, and to find out what's going on inside and outside the four walls of the company. The constraints will tell us what we cannot do, and the enablers will tell us what we can. The rest of the information will help us figure out what we should do.

To get this information, involve employees from outside of the planning team, tapping into the resources of customer-facing and supplier-facing positions. Keep in mind that in many distributor planning projects, management is too often told what they want to hear from employees, suppliers and even customers.

Assessment should be divided into two categories: Internal and External.

The Internal Environment

The assessment of a company's internal environment starts with simply gathering information. Do this all at once, rather than piecemeal, so that you have all the data required to make good decisions. This is similar to a due diligence request for a company you might want to buy: current and historical financial statements, organization charts, customer and supplier trends, details about competitors, bios of key personnel, previous strategic plans and so on. It takes a few days to assemble this information, and it takes time to analyze, but it is well worth the effort.

Finances

Financial assessment of a wholesale distribution business includes understanding the balance sheet and income statement with a special emphasis on the cash flow statement. The cash-to-cash period defines how much working capital the distributor needs to finance growth in both warehouse business and direct shipment business, which are very different. The analyst needs to determine how much growth the company's earnings can finance, as opposed to financing from suppliers (accounts payable) and from other lenders such as banks. The unused borrowing capacity of the business can be a growth enabler or a constraint. The analyst also must estimate the expected capital expenditure needs for the business. Finally, the company's income tax structure is a key part of the cash flow equation.

Your Team

How do your leaders feel about the company? The best way to find out what leaders think is to ask them privately and in person. Using an outsider to conduct these interviews has the advantage of being unbiased, as well as providing a basis for comparison with other firms. I believe in structured interviews with a short series of open-ended questions presented in a specific order. The questions are intended to open the door to serious, possibly intense conversations about the current business and options for the future. Arrange an interview for each of the people who will serve on the planning team, and possibly for others in senior positions who may not be on the team. A thorough interview will take at least one hour, if not two. Compiling interview responses must be done with care to preserve confidentiality. An outside facilitator must be discreet by scrubbing comments to protect the identities of the respondents.

For the rest of your employees, the Web provides an excellent way to do an internal environment survey. Popular survey tools like Survey Monkey (www.surveymonkey.com) are easy to use and offer increasingly powerful ways to analyze and present survey results. The results from leadership interviews are useful for tailoring employee survey questions. The survey needs to be thorough, yet short enough to finish in 45 minutes to one hour. I begin with a list of 35-40 questions that can be customized for the specific company. Use a combination of objective questions with ratings as well as open-ended essay questions. The best insights often come from the answers to the essay questions, and again care must be taken when compiling the responses to protect privacy.

Anonymity for respondents to internal surveys is a controversial subject. We have tried strategic planning surveys both ways and recommend that for most companies the best answer is anonymity for employees below the managerial level. We prefer that managers identify themselves so we can be sure that everyone is included. The gray area is outside sales reps – we want to be able to follow-up so we need identity, but the salespeople tend to be skeptical of surveys if they aren't anonymous.

Respondents should be encouraged to write as much as they wish rather than short comments. Some of my favorite essay questions are:

- What do you cherish about this company and would never change?
- Do you understand the company's strategy? Do you have confidence in it? Do you understand your role in making the strategy work?
- If you had a magic wand, what is one thing you would change immediately?
- What things would you do if you were in charge of this company?
- Is there anything else you would like to say?
- What additional questions should have been included?

CASE STUDY

Assessing the Internal Environment: Two related organizations combine planning processes, increase efficiencies

The executive staff at an international wholesale channel trade association operated two distinct entities, one made up of distributors and the other of suppliers. Traditionally, leadership of the two divisions conducted their long-range and annual planning somewhat autonomously, reflecting the sometimes-divergent goals of the body made up of distributors versus the supplier group.

The planning team recognized the strategic importance of maintaining separate entities, but at the same time saw advantages in combining the strategic planning process. The objectives were to coordinate the desired outcomes as well as better utilize staff time and other resources. The planners got critical insights from the members of each group by using a well-designed survey tool. The tool compared and contrasted responses to certain questions and obtained valuable free-form answers.

The planners were better able to identify the issues of greatest importance to each member group and to find breakthrough initiatives to meet the needs of both. The combined effort was productive, helping to make the overall organization more efficient and effective.

The External Environment

The external environment is more difficult to assess because you are getting opinions from outsiders who have little incentive to help. As a result, their responses may be unreliable or even misleading.

Customers

Recent customer satisfaction surveys or other customer feedback is useful. Most distributors don't conduct formal surveys with customers, and much of the information I get is anecdotal – interesting, but not very useful for planning strategy.

Many distributors haven't yet discovered a popular marketing tool known as the Net Promoter Score or NPS[1]. NPS sums up a customer's loyalty to a supplier in the answer to one question: "Would you recommend this supplier?" The score is tabulated by subtracting the percentage of detractors from the percentage of enthusiastic promoters. Wholesale distributors need to do a better job of tracking how their customers feel about them. But without statistically meaningful data, we must settle for what we can learn from the company's transaction database and sales analysis.

Pull three years of customer trend information from your database. Organize the following data by sales territory and by customer in a ranking report:

- sales
- gross margin dollars
- gross margin percentage
- order size
- commissions
- days sales outstanding

Keep warehouse business and direct business separate if drop ship-

---

1 For more information about NPS visit www.netpromoter.com.

ments are an important part of your business.

This analysis should yield results that show you changes in customer concentration, how many customers in each sales territory really matter and where opportunities for improvement are. You can also spot sales trends indicative of customer loyalty (or lack thereof), waning sales effectiveness and weakening of key customers. Customer Profitability Analysis (CPA) and Cost to Serve (CTS) are valuable tools for strategic analysis.[2]

Suppliers

The external environment includes both the company's suppliers, as well as the main suppliers with whom the company's suppliers compete. Suppliers are remarkably forthcoming about what is going on with their distributors, their competitors and their competitors' distributors. In fact, one of the most accessible and objective sources of information about a company may be the right person at a large supplier.

Suppliers also have excellent insights on coming changes in the marketplace, especially if their sales force is alert and has clear communication channels to upper management. Savvy supplier sales reps pick up signals about the shifting marketplace from their conversations with distributor managers and sales reps, as well as from end-user visits. Actions in an isolated market may indicate what another manufacturer or large distributor plans to do elsewhere.

Competitors

Thanks to the Web, information about competitors is increasingly easy to obtain. However, there is a big gap between collecting competitive information and knowing what it means and what to do with it. For now, a few hours with search engines and social networking sites such as LinkedIn and even Facebook can provide a handy profile of other distributors including names and background information about

---

2 For more on these concepts, see my book *In Search of the Perfect Customer.* Published by National Association of Wholesaler-Distributors, 2011.

CASE STUDY

Supplier Assessment:
Safety distributor identifies and closes
strategy gaps with key suppliers

A specialized distributor of safety products was experiencing great friction in three of its key supplier relationships. In one case the company was among the nation's largest distributors for a critical vendor, yet the supplier threatened to cancel the distributor's exclusivity in its market segment. Management wanted to salvage the relationships.

The team identified strategy gaps between the distributor and the suppliers. An outside facilitator's meeting with the suppliers without the distributor present revealed the root causes of the problems. Vendor executives felt the distributor's increasingly inflexible market approach was out of step with the market and with the suppliers' goals.

The planning team concluded that two of the vendors' products and new technologies were the key to the distributor's distinctive value proposition and to the future growth of the firm.

As a result the company changed its product emphasis and selling approach to better align with two of the three vendors. Data showed that the third vendor's products were not profitable and the vendor was dropped.

their sales forces and support staff. Useful financial information about competitors may be amazingly easy to obtain. With some digging and careful analysis, you can sketch out a fairly clear picture of what your competitors' strategies are and how they are working out.

The Playing Field

Now that you have gathered this information, it is time to take a step back and get each business unit involved in analyzing the state of your business. Jack Welch devoted a whole chapter of his popular book *Winning*[3] to the importance of analyzing the business playing field. "Neutron Jack" explains the demands he made on his executives at General Electric to make playing field presentations at management meetings. GE is known for its rigorous accountability.

The playing field metaphor works. It is easy for most people to visualize a marketplace of customers, suppliers and competitors as a space used for games. The distributor teams are lined up in a grand contest, the object of which is to align with the best suppliers and win the customers' profitable business.

Welch's playing field analysis is a powerful tool. The opportunity to present a short but information-packed analysis of what's going on in their own areas of the business makes operating executives an integral part of planning. Even if managers aren't on the planning team, they will feel like a part of the process. Ideally managers will present to the planning team in person.

Each business unit should cover the following five questions. Under each question, they should list critical changes to the customer base, among sales reps, and with suppliers, products and services.

I adapted the following playing field questions from Welch's book.

---

3 See *Winning* by Jack Welch with Suzy Welch. Published by HarperBusiness, 2005.

Chapter 3 - Assessment of the Status Quo

What has changed on my business unit's playing field since the last planning session?

Think of the external environment in macroeconomic terms: GDP growth, inflation, unemployment and interest rates. Consider the effect of mergers and acquisitions, as well as financial failure of customers, suppliers and competitors. Reflect on the impact of population shifts, immigration, company relocations and plant openings and closings.

What has the competition done to change my playing field?

Review openings and closings of regional distribution centers, branches and retail locations. For distributors, adding sales reps and technical support staff can be critical. Adding and subtracting product lines and suppliers, as well as services, can dramatically affect the playing field. For distributors, well-executed technology investments make a real difference.

What have I done to change the playing field during that time?

Some moves help you and hurt the opponents at the same time, such as securing competitors' top salespeople and key product lines. Increasing penetration at major accounts and capturing competitors' accounts increases share and harpoons other distributors in the market. Successful implementation of new technologies and business processes can also make a big difference on the playing field.

What am I planning to do in the next 12 months?

The planning team needs to know what moves are already planned for the coming 12 months. Business unit managers can't sit back while awaiting the outcomes of the strategic planning project. They are lining up new suppliers, targeting customers and pieces of business, and recruiting salespeople.

What devastating news might I get in the next 12 months?

Business unit managers need to grapple with potential bad news that could hurt the company in the coming months. Some people call this scenario planning. What would we do if we lost a critical product line?

CASE STUDY

Unearthing Weaknesses:
Fluid power distributor diversifies supplier base & expands footprint through acquisitions

A large regional distributor of fluid power products identified that one of its weaknesses was that it was heavily dependent on one supplier. Management wanted to diversify its revenue stream by growing rapidly in newer products.

The planning team identified compatible product lines and geographic markets. Management understood that they did not have the capacity or patience to use a "scattershot" approach or to waste time on the wrong prospects. Using an acquisitions criteria filter, the company evaluated acquisition candidates. They pinpointed targets with the best strategic fit and likelihood of deal success.

As a result the company made five acquisitions in five years, significantly increasing sales and profits. Ironically the expanded territories provided attractive opportunities for growth with the major vendor. The major supplier is still extremely important; however, management feels more comfortable now with a bigger geographic footprint and diversified sources of revenue.

View an example of the acquisitions filter this distributor used on the next page.

Figure 3-1: Acquisitions Filter

Agreement on acquisition criteria is the first step in launching a successful acquisitions program. The discipline of establishing and following criteria prevents wasting time on targets that don't fit into a strategic plan. Is the target big enough to "move the needle"? Is it affordable without unacceptable risk? Do the product lines, services and customer segments fit into the company's strategy? Would integration take too long or be too risky? Besides the "laundry list" in the chart, other criteria might be customer and/or vendor concentration, median sales force age or management depth. The acquisitions filter is helpful if the distributor decides to use professional assistance to find targets.

Target Characteristics	Consider	Ideal	Will not consider
Sales revenue	Under $10M	$10M-$20M	Over $20M
Cultural fit	Good fit	Good fit	Not a good fit
Profitability	No turnarounds	No turnarounds	Turnaround situations
Price	Under $3M	$3M-$6M	Over $6M
Location	Within current markets	Adjacent markets	Outside adjacent markets
Customer segments	Reasonably compatible	Compatible	Not compatible
Product lines	Same as ours	Mostly same as ours	Competing lines
Value-added services (VAS)	Service and assembly	Service and assembly	No VAS
CEO commitment to remain	Stay 6-12 months	Stay 12-36 months	Leave immediately
Outside sales representative	Non-compete agreements	Non-compete agreements	Not under contract
ERP system	Same as ours; older version	Same as ours; older version	Other systems
Real estate	Short-term lease	Medium-term lease	Will not purchase

How would we manage the loss of a major customer or a key sales rep?

Allocating about three minutes to each slide, take 15 minutes for each presentation plus time to answer questions. The business unit presentations give any outside members of the planning team a good sense of each business unit and the strengths and weaknesses of business unit managers.

Here are some examples of what different business units may present in a Playing Field session:

A vice president of sales may talk about competition, especially the efforts of other companies to recruit top sales reps away from competitors. He may analyze the opening and closing of competitor branch locations and how those moves create both opportunities and challenges for the company.

A purchasing director may review product lines carried by competitors including lines they had taken on and given up on. A purchasing director may have several examples of potentially desirable product lines that may be willing to consider the company as a distributor. Purchasing may also analyze the benefits the company receives from its buying group compared with other groups that competitors belong to.

The CFO may show the distributor's financial trends over the past three years, including improvements in cash flow cycle, receivables collection and vendor payables, reduction of bank debt, faster inventory turnover and availability of borrowing capacity for expansion. He may also assess the relative financial strength of the company's competitors.

An operations manager may analyze the logistics advantages and disadvantages of competitors as compared with one another and to the company itself.

The IT director may breakdown competitors' IT and electronic commerce capabilities.

SWOT Analysis

A SWOT analysis is the bridge from the assessment phase to the brainstorming of initiatives. Personal interviews and survey results, as well as the playing field presentations, can yield rich information about a distributor's strengths, weaknesses, opportunities and threats, or SWOT.

This analysis can be compiled on a sheet of paper with four color-coded columns. Each of the elements – S, W, O and T – can be lined up op-

Figure 3-2: SWOT (Strength, Weakness, Opportunity, Threat) Matrix

This matrix shows the value of lining up categories across the four SWOT columns. In some categories the distributor may have both a strength and a weakness. It is sometimes hard to see that the same topic presents both a threat and an opportunity. Distributors need to build on their strengths and avoid their weaknesses, unless they are determined to turn that weakness around.

Strengths	Weaknesses	Opportunities	Threats
major supplier	buy-back dependency	more special relationships	cancellation
customer relationships		lead generation	loss of local presence/value
scale	not delivering more value		
technology		get software working	
experienced top management	leadership spread out		inflexibility of shareholders
logistics	slow response		
strong technical sales force	sales drop-off	strengthen sales force	
	lack of pricing power	strategic pricing	margin deterioration
	electronic commerce	website	

posite other elements that relate directly to it. For example, a strength may be the distributor's exclusive relationship with a huge supplier. A related weakness may be dependence on that supplier due to its lack of predictability. Perhaps a related threat is that the supplier could appoint other distributors in its market or sell out to a competitor. Finally, a related opportunity is to reduce dependence on that supplier by diversification or expansion into other products.

This analysis points to strengths you can exploit and weaknesses to avoid. It also identifies threats to anticipate and prepare to defend against, as well as opportunities to attack.

✅ STRATEGY CHECKPOINT

Use these questions to further assess the status of your business. Some of these questions require you to do some hands-on research – talk to and survey your employees and management teams. They also require you to be candid with yourself and your team about past challenges related to planning.

1. How did your people react to the news that the company is undertaking a strategic planning project? If the response was less than enthusiastic, or even apathetic, have previous planning efforts been poorly communicated or badly executed? Is the staff skeptical that management is truly committed to making major changes if needed?

2. How do your people feel about having the opportunity to participate in planning through completion of an in-depth survey? If they aren't "amped up" is it because previous surveys have not resulted in needed changes or even feedback of the survey results?

3. How much time does the management team spend talking about the future, both informally and in meetings? Is most or all of the discussion about the problems of the day?

4. Does the team hold itself accountable for meeting sales forecasts, expense budgets and customer service metrics? What action is taken when performance is below expectations?

5. What is the company's track record in execution of large projects? How are managers held accountable for what is assigned to them and for meeting agreed-upon deadlines? How well do the individuals pull together as a team?

6. Does your distribution business consist of business units that are discrete parts of your operation, somewhat independent of one another?

If so, how do you organize the leadership of the business units?

7. If you embrace the idea of strategic business units (SBUs), how are your SBU leaders held responsible for their strategic moves, as well as their tactical activities?

8. How much time does the management team devote to discussing strategic moves at the SBU level, such as hiring new sales reps, opening new locations, or recruiting critical product lines and key players away from the competition?

9. How often does the team talk about what developments could cause serious harm to the business, and what contingency plans should be in place?

Chapter 4
The Driving Force

One of the first steps in strategic planning is to identify and understand your company's driving force.

The distributor's driving force connects the leader's vision for the business with the compelling goal (see Chapter 6 for more on this) that the strategic planning group develops. The driving force is a way of thinking about the business, and for many it's a new way of thinking.

I first read about the idea of a business driving force in a book called *Strategy Pure & Simple* by Michel Robert.[1] Robert explained his view that there is one particular force that drives a company's profit. For example, the driving force of an oil exploration company is its natural resources; for a high-tech company, the force is technology. Apple's driving force is clear – design. The driving force for Amazon.com, which in 2012 launched AmazonSupply.com to compete more directly with industrial and lab supplies distributors, is its selling method. The Home Shopping Network is another example of a company whose proprietary selling method drives profit.

Naturally I wanted to see how the driving force idea applies to wholesale distribution companies.

The selling method is of prime importance to distribution businesses. Many distributors are proud of their sales function. But the sales method, however effective, is not distinctive enough to be a driving force for

---

1 See *Strategy Pure & Simple* by Michel Robert. Published by McGraw-Hill Inc., 1993.

the typical distributor.

Logistics may seem to be a strong candidate. However, warehousing and delivery techniques for most distributors aren't distinguishing enough to be considered a driving force. The examples of logistics in Robert's book are unique distribution capabilities such as Walmart and McDonald's – businesses that can push a wide variety of products through remarkably efficient systems.

So which characteristic of most wholesale distribution businesses is the "point of the spear" – the singular force that makes profit happen? If that force isn't the sales or distribution methods, what could it be?

We've posed this driving force question to CEOs and groups of managers at numerous distribution companies.

Planning Tip

A driving force discussion is an excellent small group breakout topic at a strategic planning retreat. Even within the same company people have very different ideas about what the company's driving force is.

A surprisingly large percentage identifies "making money" as the top candidate. But this again does not fit for distribution companies. Generating profits is the driving force for companies in the financial world – such as a hedge fund charged with generating high returns for its clients. You may ask: "Why isn't this the case for distributors?" My response is a paraphrase of Peter Drucker's answer to a similar question: "You are not in the business of making money; you are in the business of distributing tires (or widgets, etc.)."

For most distributors, the driving force is either an extraordinary knowledge of product applications or a remarkably deep understanding of their customers' needs.

Exceptional product application capabilities are the profit engine for the former. These distributors may know more about their product features than their suppliers do, and they have superior insights into how the products are used by their customers. They are technically savvy problem-solvers. These distributors seek to find as many potential users of their products as possible.

The other group is driven by uncommon knowledge of their customers' businesses and product needs. These distributors are able to anticipate what their customers' needs will be and adjust their products and services offerings accordingly. These distributors seek to fulfill as many of their customers' needs as they can.

There are notable exceptions to the above. National MRO distributor W.W. Grainger has built a distribution system that is comparable with Walmart in retailing and McDonald's in fast food. The highly developed and proprietary Grainger system is capable of distributing a wide assortment of products. As a result, Grainger has been able to expand its product portfolio aggressively.

The importance of identifying and agreeing on the driving force early in the strategic planning process is critical before trying to articulate a business concept (Chapter 5) and outline initiatives (Chapter 9). In most cases, management needs to accept that the company's logistics, technology and sales methods are probably not that much better or different from their competitors'.

When you resolve the driving force question between product application knowledge and understanding of customer needs you will be better prepared to design your strategy. For one thing, the "What's more important: customers or suppliers?" question gets answered.

Product application distributors tend to be focused more on suppliers. Distributors dominated by a major supplier know who they are, but they need to recognize that their key supplier's strategy is an irresistible influence in determining their own. They are technically oriented problem-solvers, and they line up their resources and initiatives accordingly. They generally have a larger number of smaller customers.

Customer needs-focused distributors concentrate their forces on penetrating their customers more deeply, taking full advantage of each precious customer relationship. They usually have a smaller number of larger customers.

Leadership Discipline

Changing the subject from driving force for distributors, I want you to think about whether you need to focus your company's strategy on excelling in operations, customer intimacy or both. By customer intimacy I am not referring simply to an understanding of customer business needs. Consider the vital role played by your sales force in forging close personal relationships with the people in your customers' organizations.

Harvard Business School's famed Michael Porter wrote the classic *Competitive Strategy: Techniques for Analyzing Industries and Competitors*[2] in 1980. His seminal book boils strategy down to three options: cost leadership, differentiation or market segmentation. Porter argues for focus on one, but only one, of his dimensions.

In a more recent book, *The Discipline of Market Leaders: Choose Your Customers, Narrow Your Focus, Dominate Your Market*[3], authors Michael Treacy and Fred Wiersema adapted the three Porter strategies into a choice of customer intimacy, operational excellence or product leadership. If you agree that product leadership isn't a viable option for most distributors, the authors leave distributors with two alternatives: operational excellence or customer intimacy. In the following paragraphs I will argue for a third option.

---

2 See *Competitive Strategy: Techniques for Analyzing Industries and Competitors*, by Michael Porter. Published by Harvard Business Press.

3 Distributors relate very well to the idea of differentiation, expanded on in a clear and practical way in a 1990s bestseller by Michael Treacy and Fred Wiersema, *The Discipline of Market Leaders: Choose Your Customers, Narrow Your Focus, Dominate Your Market*. Published by HarperCollins Publishers Inc.

Strategic choice No. 1 in *The Discipline of Market Leaders* is operational excellence, keeping costs down while making the customer's life easier. It embodies being fast and efficient, eliminating redundancies in the channel, avoiding mistakes, delivering just-in-time and so on. Operationally excellent distributors use metrics to manage their businesses, monitor and control their processes, and strive to improve quality and minimize costs. In the interest of efficiency, these distributors encourage their customers to accept a limited assortment of products and service options.

Strategic choice No. 2, customer intimacy, as defined by Treacy and Wiersema, is exemplified by distributors that are extremely close to their customers and are eager to customize their business processes and services to strengthen the relationship.

The Discipline of Market Leaders states that the demands on financial resources and management time make it unrealistic to try to focus on more than one of the basic value disciplines. The authors contend that failure to focus on one value only results in lack of market differentiation and poor results. They argue the need to go "past operational competence to reach operational excellence" and "past customer responsiveness to create customer intimacy."

I disagree about these values being mutually exclusive for distributors. Our experience with strategic planning for distributors demonstrates that operational excellence is no longer optional – it's a requirement. Operational excellence is taken for granted by the customers distributors want most.

Customer expectations have risen markedly since the Treacy and Wiersema book was published in 1993. Distributor gross margins in most lines of trade have lost ground in recent years. There is less room for bloated operating costs. Both from the vantage of customer expectations and operating margins, mere operational competence is not enough to compete for business and make adequate profits.

Using the language of *The Discipline of Market Leaders*, what we see as the imperative of operational excellence would leave customer intimacy as the only choice of discipline for wholesale distributors. Not only do we see the operational excellence as compatible with customer intimacy, for distributors we see them as inseparable. They are interdependent, and they are both essential.

Let me take that one step further: Customer intimacy equals operational excellence for wholesale distributors. We have left the age of mass markets. In the words of Jonathan Byrnes[4], senior lecturer at MIT, we have entered the age of precision markets. Distributors make most of their operating profits from a small number of large customers (and most lose a good amount of those profits doing business with a handful of large customers).

The discipline of customer intimacy requires you to be close with your major accounts at multiple levels. The discipline of operational excellence mandates that you align all aspects of your operation to the current (and foreseeable) needs of your most profitable accounts. Helping your best customers increase their profit makes both you and your customers more effective and efficient.

If every distributor chose customer intimacy as the basis of its business strategy, how would the individual businesses be distinguishable from one another? What could the companies do to be distinctive in the eyes of their customers? Could we jump to the conclusion that all distributors are simply trying to do the same thing – be intimate with their customers – but some execute better than the others?

If every distributor knows how to get operational excellence right (a faulty assumption of course) you might surmise that they all look alike to customers, and the only difference from one company to another is price. That is a scary notion, and we need to negate it. Execution is so

---

4 See *Islands of Profit in a Sea of Red Ink: Why 40 Percent of Your Business is Unprofitable and How to Fix It*, by Jonathan L. S. Byrnes. Published by Portfolio Hardcover, 2010.

difficult that even if every competitor pursued identical strategies there would be major differences from one company to another.

Answer these questions to help you understand driving force. Again, you will need to be honest about your capabilities, as well as what your customers truly value.

1. How does your team react to interdependence of customer intimacy and operational excellence for a distributor? Would the group rather choose one over the other?

2. What is the team's attitude about the statement that product leadership for most distributors is not a primary discipline?

3. How does your sales force stack up against your direct competitors? Most distributors are justifiably proud of their sales forces and correctly view their sales efforts as a primary reason for their success. Even if you feel your sales group is superior to the competition, how does your sales method differ? Is it proprietary in any way?

4. Logistics capabilities are a hallmark for many distributors. How does your logistics competency compare to the competition? Is your logistics method different? How is it proprietary?

5. Many distributors have made large investments in technology such as high-level ERP systems, warehouse management and truck routing software, and e-commerce tools. How does your technology capability compare to the competition? Is your technology method different from the competition? Is it proprietary?

Chapter 5
The Business Concept & Elevator Speech

A business concept is the product of your culture and traditions, as well as strategic decisions about your markets. A business concept is a reflection of where the company has been, how it has evolved and what has made it successful.

Do two things with your business concept. First, put it into words in such a straightforward way that everyone in the company knows what it is. Second, make sure the concept reflects not only where the company has been but where you want it to go.

Why do customers buy from you rather than a competitor? What is truly distinctive about your value proposition?

The business concept for distributors will determine how you deploy your people's time.

A manufacturer is more focused on how the company uses its capital to build plants and buy machinery. A retailer concentrates more on where stores are located and how advertising dollars are used. The distributor's choices are what to sell, where to sell and to whom. For distributors, one-third of the workforce is typically higher-paid salespeople. You only have the capacity to have a finite number of salespeople in the field, and they have a set number of hours each year to generate sales. The utilization of that sales capacity is as critical to a distributor as use of production capacity is for a manufacturer or sales per square foot is for a retailer. What is not used effectively is forever lost.

The sales cycle time varies dramatically from one group of customers to another.

I divide customers and prospects into four groups:

Auctioneers are interested only in getting the lowest price. Their business is easiest to get – just offer them a hot price – and naturally it's easiest to lose to a starving competitor. That business is also the least desirable as it is low margin and isn't sticky.

Figure 5-1: Four Types of Customers

The four customer types are a useful way to start the all-important discussion about how many and what types of salespeople you need. Many distributors have too many sales reps and may not have the right mix. The best way to frame the debate is to consider which types of customers will get the distributor to where the planning team wants to go.

Negotiators	Partners
• Decision made by department manager • Short-term agreement • Preferred supplier for one or more categories • Loose evaluation criteria – annual review • Some switching costs and risk • Problem-solving teams when needed • Longer selling cycle; access can be difficult • Hunter-type sales executive	• Decision made in executive suite • Long-term agreement • Exclusive supplier for multiple categories • Strict evaluation criteria – periodic review • High switching costs and risk • Multidisciplinary teams on both sides • Long selling cycle; access difficult • Boardroom-level sales executive
Auctioneers	**Wheeler Dealers**
• Decision made by buyer • Purchase orders or bids • Recognized as acceptable supplier • No performance review • No switching costs or risk • No selling cycle; access easy • Rookie sales rep, inside sales or direct contact	• Decision made by a purchasing manager • Blanket orders • Approved supplier for one or more categories • Complaints when demands not met • No switching costs or risk • Problem-solving by sales rep when needed • Shorter selling cycle; access not difficult • Farmer-type sales rep

Chapter 5 - The Business Concept & Elevator Speech

Wheeler Dealers want a low price but they also want decent service. They are harder to please and will pay a bit more than price-only customers. It takes somewhat longer to get their orders, and they are more loyal, but their business isn't that coveted.

Negotiators are interested in getting a good price, but their objective is more holistic. They want good service, but they also look for the maximum overall value: product quality, selection, advice. They are more loyal and their business is much more sought after even though the selling cycle is much longer.

Partners are searching for suppliers who can help them solve their problems. They want to partner with the smartest suppliers who will ultimately assist them in making the most money by saving time, eliminating waste and increasing satisfaction for their customers. Even though the selling cycle is very long, every distributor wants these customers because they are the most loyal. Some suppliers don't have what it takes to capture these accounts, and they will never get them – or if they do, they won't keep them for long.

I discuss these segments and how to choose which to target in Chapter 8 – The Sweet Spot: Selecting Investments.

The utilization of the distributor sales force and support staff is the allocation of their time to go after each of the groups outlined above. It is a primary strategic decision. If no direction is provided, the sales reps will make these decisions for themselves based on their own skills and perceptions.

An Analogy: Salespeople as Assets

Think of each salesperson as an asset that is not actually on the balance sheet but maybe should be. I estimate the dollars invested in a new distributor salesperson to get him to the point of becoming a profit generator, which sometimes takes two or three years, at more than $150,000. If distributors capitalized these costs as one would a piece of production equipment – instead of writing if off as a current expense – that would be an asset on the balance sheet of at least $150,000 per salesperson. Ten sales reps at a location would be $1.5 million.

Figure 5-2: Cost of Recruiting and Developing a New Outside Distributor Sales Representative

The cost of developing top sales talent is the biggest investment for most distributors. It also carries the greatest degree of risk. Distributor strategic planning almost invariably delves into sales force attraction, development and retention. The crucial nature of these decisions makes them strategic for distributors. The "brutal facts" are that most distributors depend on their top salespeople for growth, that such people are costly and the success rate is often too low.

	Upfront	Ongoing cost (2 years)	Total cost incurred during recruiting and development phase
Advertising, interviews, transportation, placement fees	Placement $12,000; other $5,000	NA	$17,000
Relocation, orientation, equipment, legal fees	Relo $25,000 Other $10,000	NA	$35,000
Training	20 training days @ $400	12 training days in first year @ $400	$12,800
Compensation & benefits during development phase	NA	$60,000 base + 25% fringes; 5% raise after 12 months	$75,000 year 1; $78,750 year 2
Less: commissions generated during development phase	NA	Ramp up by $2,000/quarter after first quarter	$12,000 year 1; $44,000 year 2
Expense reimbursement during development phase	NA	$500/month	$12,000
Sales management, coaching & supervision during development phase	NA	12 hours/month @ $50 per hour	$14,400
TOTAL (2 years)			$188,950

Chapter 5 - The Business Concept & Elevator Speech

CASE STUDY

Allocating Salespeople's Time: Industrial distributor redeploys sales force, boosts accountability

A distributor of industrial and other chemical products had two major product groups, one growing rapidly but the other in steady decline. Management wanted to emphasize building the fast-growing line without losing ground in the other products.

The planners used in-depth interviews with managers and surveys of the sales force to gain a clearer picture of how the sales force was operating with customers of the distinctly different product lines. The planning team identified strategic opportunities to redeploy the sales force and improve sales team accountability. The sellers were assigned one customer segment in which they would specialize in customer application needs and product requirements. The sales team was divided into smaller groups to provide a high level of accountability for results.

As a result the smaller team of specialists handling the mature products strengthened their position in a shrinking market. The larger team of reps calling on the fast-growth segments gained market share from competitors.

Those dollars are just as much an asset as machinery and equipment is to a manufacturer. If the sales rep were depreciated over 10 years the annual depreciation would be $15,000. If a sales rep walked out the door the loss would be the remaining book value. The hypothetical sales book value makes up a portion of the goodwill of the business, representing part of the future profits the company expects the salesperson to generate.

I hope this accounting analogy got your attention. Now visualize the sales rep book value as an asset on the balance sheet and compare the capacity each person has to the capacity of a manufacturer's production equipment.

Each salesperson can make so many sales calls in a given period, let's say a year. Each year has 2,080 potential selling hours (52 weeks times 40 hours), less holidays and vacations, sales meetings and other meetings. Some of that time will be spent checking and responding to messages, filling out reports and doing clerical work such as routine pricing. With any luck, there will be 600 or 700 hours left to spend with customers building relationships, selling ideas and solving problems.

Where will they spend that valuable time? This is where your business concept comes into play.

Part One of your business concept defines what customer segments you want to attack, what products and services you want to sell and what geographic markets you want to be in.

Part Two of your business concept states why your customers buy from you and not one of your many competitors.

The universe of competitors includes other distributors, manufacturers selling direct, catalogs and other direct mail, Internet sellers, warehouse clubs and retailers. Do they choose your company because your prices are the lowest? Is your inventory the broadest and/or the deepest? Are your locations the most convenient? Do you have the best brands? Do you have the fastest delivery? Does your company have the best technical support? Do you have the finest repair and maintenance department in the market? Are your salespeople the top problem-solvers?

The Elevator Speech

After you have developed your business concept, you are ready to write your company's elevator speech. An elevator speech in the classic sense explains the business in just a few words. A really good elevator speech creates a lasting impression by saying something memorable, maybe even something exciting, about the company.

I ask distributor staff how they would describe the business to a neighbor at a picnic, or better yet how they would explain it to a 12-year-old. Even great salespeople sometimes fumble with this. It is harder to write a short letter than a long one, and it's more challenging to come up with an elevator speech than a lengthy explanation. The short message must be clear, jargon-free and have punch. The content must be presented so that the listener understands and remembers. Mere slogans don't work.

Here's an example of an elevator speech describing a business concept:

We carry the broadest and deepest inventory of products for widget industry professionals with immediate availability of over 12,000 items from more than 10 convenient locations.

When doing this with a group, I use an exercise modeled after the popular missing-word game MadLibs. It gets the planning group to focus on the content rather than the form by starting with two simple sentences and a few blank spaces to add words.

The words to be inserted in the blanks can be restricted to a list provided by the facilitator, but I prefer that the list be offered only as suggestions or thought-starters.

Here is an example of this exercise:

Apex ____A____ ____B____ to ____C____ in ____D____.
Our customers buy from us because we ____E____ , ____F____ and ____G____ better.

A – what we do (supply, design, build …)
B – what we provide (products, services, information …)
C – who buys from us
D – where they are
E, F, G – things we do that are distinctive

✅ STRATEGY CHECKPOINT

Use these questions to start a discussion over whether your company makes decisions and allocates resources based on where you want to do business.

1. Does your sales force spend enough of its time patiently building business with Negotiators and Partners? Can you see a pattern in which the strongest sellers invest time in accounts that require a long-term effort while others always go after the business that offers immediate gratification? Do some of your sellers gravitate toward buyers and purchasing agents, avoiding selling to management?

2. Do you jealousy protect the 600-700 prime selling hours that each of your sellers has each year? Is the business structured to enable the sales force to spend as much time as possible in front of the people at the best prospects and customers, building relationships and selling concepts and solving problems? Does the strategy make it crystal clear where they need to be spending time and what they must be focused on?

3. Do the people in your company know why your top customers prefer to do business with you rather than your many competitors? Do they understand why your best suppliers choose to go to market through your firm rather than some other way? Does your management team know why your best employees joined your company and why they stay with you?

4. Could your employees explain what your company does to a neighbor or friend in a short, compelling and memorable way?

Chapter 6

The Compelling Goal & Growth Trajectory

John F. Kennedy's legendary challenge to put an American on the moon by the end of the 1960s is a great example of what Jim Collins[1] coined a "big hairy audacious goal," or BHAG. A well-known example from the corporate world is the Lexus BHAG: "Beat Mercedes."[2]

What about your business can inspire your people like this?

Don't confuse a BHAG, or Compelling Goal, with a company mission statement. I am not opposed to having a mission statement, but they tend to be bland and most contain the same hopeful catchphrases:

- Exceed customer expectations.
- Be the dominant supplier. (I hate this one – what customer wants to be dominated by his suppliers?)
- Be a great place to work.
- Be the supplier of choice.

The overall effect is uninspiring and mostly meaningless to employees. The mission statements I refer to here are also undefined: How will I know if we accomplished our mission? What does it mean to me?

To be compelling, your goal needs to connect with your employees' emotions. The criteria for a "SMART" goal are: specific, measurable,

---

1 See *Built to Last: Successful Habits of Visionary Companies*, by Jim Collins and Jerry I. Porras. Published by HarperBusiness, 1995.

2 See *Good to Great: Why Some Companies Make the Leap … and Others Don't*, Jim Collins. Published by HarperBusiness, 2001.

actionable, realistic, time-sensitive. The goal doesn't need to contain a specific deadline but it must at least imply a sense of urgency. When Lexus said "Beat Mercedes" they were describing something concrete and measurable: Sell more luxury cars in the U.S. than the well-established leader at the time.

Lexus had to demonstrate to its people that the goal was realistic and dependent on the actions of the individuals and their teams within Lexus. The urgency was implied: If we don't do it, some other car company may get there before we do. (BMW? Audi? Infiniti?) It was certainly not obvious that Lexus was going to become so outrageously successful.

For distributors, deciding on a Big Hairy Audacious Goal, as Collins puts it, may be perplexing. The choices are mostly limited to shooting for a revenue level, becoming the largest distributor for a particularly important brand or product line, or surpassing a competitor. Distribution tends to be a market-by-market business in which a company may be a winner in one geographic area but an also-ran in others.

For a distributor, reaching a much higher revenue level is the easiest to measure, and because of this is a common choice. But a negative of a revenue-based goal is that employees may easily see why growing sales is good for the shareholders, but it may not be exciting for them. Setting a goal in dollars suggests that it's all about money, and the staff may reasonably expect a monetary reward when the goal is reached.

A market share-based goal works especially well if the distributor has a defining, premier product line (Budweiser, Caterpillar, Parker Hannifin or Allen-Bradley for example). Setting the company's sights on a target of becoming the largest distributor in its markets, assuming that the line isn't exclusive, or being in the top 10 in the country, can be a SMART goal and is usually accompanied by recognition from the supplier. A celebration may be in order.

Knowing that you have beaten a competitor, however, may be difficult due to lack of market share data. But there may be useful indicators such as acquiring the competitor, their withdrawal from the market, or the capture of a critical product line or customer.

One of our distributor clients came up with a creative BHAG that focuses entirely on employees: to become one of the top companies to work for in its state. A business magazine runs a contest each year with objective criteria to identify the winners, making it possible to measure success. Another distributor drove its goal with a quality imperative: become the first distributor in its market to earn a quality designation (such as QS-9000).

Consulting firm McKinsey & Company identifies three essential in-gredients for strategic plan execution: a compelling goal, role clarity for each employee and trust based on strong communication. To make the BHAG real, management must create awareness and understand-ing, and support the goal consistently and sincerely. Jack Welch[3] at GE launched the Six Sigma quality initiative and stuck with it as a primary corporate goal for several years while it was driven throughout his empire.

Once you are committed to your goal, a strong and consistent message from leadership at all levels is required. The staff wants to know: Where are we going? Why are we going there? How will we get there? When will we get there? What will happen when we get there? What do you want me to do?

Your goal may or may not be focused on a revenue target, or even on growth specifically. I do however want the planning team to settle on a growth trajectory for the business, to help in understanding where your company will be over the next few years and how that could affect how you operate your business.

---

3 See *Winning* by Jack Welch with Suzy Welch. Published by HarperBusiness, 2005.

Chapter 6 - The Compelling Goal & Growth Trajectory

One of the ways we keep score in business is sales revenue dollars. Years ago many distributors considered their sales to be a closely guarded secret, as if the employees would not understand (they may have been right about that) or that the information would be valuable to competitors or suppliers (they were most likely wrong about that). Many distributors declined to provide sales data to the Dun & Bradstreet credit reporting service. Some would not even reveal their sales amount to their trade associations, a problem because the dues level is often based on company size.

Now that more distributors are less secretive about their results, even introducing elements of open book management, more employees know their companies' revenue. One of the products of the planning process is Key Performance Indicators (more on that in Chapter 7). The starting point is sales revenue.

Validating Your Goal Growth Rate

As stated earlier, oftentimes a distributor's compelling goal is to achieve a certain level of sales growth. The company's goal, for example, may call for the doubling of sales within 10 years. You may know the "Rule of 72," which states that the result of dividing the number 72 by the number of years, 10 in this example, indicates the compound growth rate needed – here about 7%.

The planning team needs to validate that the distributor is capable of financing the targeted growth rate.

This exercise has three parts.

1. How much working capital will be needed to finance the growth plan?
2. Will the business generate enough profits to meet the growing company's cash needs?
3. If profits don't provide enough capital to sustain growth, is the company's balance sheet strong enough to support more debt? In

other words, would a bank lend the company the money needed to bankroll the expected growth?

The working capital needs of the distribution business depend on two factors: the relative proportion of warehouse sales and direct shipment sales, and the operating cycle. Depending on the payment terms of the distributor's suppliers, the working capital investment required to support direct shipments is less than warehouse sales because directs don't require an investment in inventory. In some cases the distributor's customer may pay the invoice even before the distributor has to pay his supplier.

Warehouse sales usually require significant working capital, depending on the operating cycle. The operating cycle is the "cash-to-cash" waiting period between the date when the distributor pays his supplier and the distributor receives payment from his customer.

For example, a distributor:

- turns inventory over 6 times a year for an average inventory carrying period of 60 days;
- gets paid by customers in 50 days; and
- must pay the supplier in 20 days.

The operating cycle then is 90 days: (60 days + 50 days) – 20 days. There are about four, 90-day periods per year.

If most transactions are warehouse sales, a distributor with a 90-day operating cycle turns cash over four times per year. Each dollar of warehouse sales growth requires (at selling price) about 25 cents of working capital. If the business is growing steadily, this cash is permanently invested in the inventory and receivables needed to carry the increased volume of warehouse business.

Distributor capital needs aren't limited to financing working capital.

Figure 6-1: Distributor Operating Cycle

The distributor operating cycle describes how long it takes to turn a cash investment in inventory into cash received from customers. The length of the cycle depends on product lead times, vendor payment terms, inventory turnover and customer payment habits. The longer the operating cycle, the more net working capital is needed to run the business. The more working capital is required, the more cash is needed. The operating cycle varies greatly among various lines of trade and among distributors within a given trade line.

	Example A	Example B	Example C
Receivables	40 days	50 days	30 days
Inventory	60 days	70 days	35 days
Payables	30 days	20 days	35 days
Operating Cycle	70 days	100 days	30 days
Per $1 Growth	$0.20	$0.35	$0.08

Eventually, incremental business creates a need for major capital expenditures such as warehouse space and equipment, delivery equipment and information systems.

Ideally the distributor's cash flow is adequate to finance growing sales. As Warren Buffett[4] puts it: "To a business, cash is like oxygen. When you have enough you never think about it. When you don't have enough, it's the only thing you can think about." Cash is king.

The three variables for cash flow are:
1. how profitable the business is
2. how much of the profit is being reinvested
3. how fast the business is growing

A business that is not earning and reinvesting profits can't finance even a slow growth rate. The cash demands of rapid growth can outstrip the reinvested cash flow of even a robustly profitable distributor.

---

4 Berkshire Hathaway Inc. annual letter from Warren Buffett to shareholders, March 2011.

To compute how much growth the distributor can finance, divide after-tax profits by net working capital. For example, a distributor has:

- receivables of $3 million
- inventory of $2 million
- accounts payable of $1 million.

Net working capital is $4 million (3 + 2 - 1).

If after-tax profits are $500,000 and all of that cash is reinvested, the equation to determine how much growth can be financed looks like this:

After-tax profits	$500,000
Divided by: Net working capital	$4 million
Equals	12.5%

The distribution business in this example generates enough after-tax cash flow to sustain an annual growth rate of 12.5% out of its earnings, if all the cash is reinvested in the business and there are no capital expenditures.

The management team must understand and accept the financial limitations on their company's growth rate. In the above example, the working capital demands of rapid growth would put a damper on capital expenditures. Hiring of new employees needed to support the growth would be severely constrained if the immediate cost of the new hires caused after-tax earnings to fall below the $500,000 needed to finance working capital growth. Virtually any such expenditure would necessitate borrowing that the company might be unwilling or unable to undertake.

When the reinvested cash flow isn't adequate the company needs to find other sources of working capital. One of the options is for the owners to make a capital infusion – an additional investment or a loan to the company. The need for cash may pop up unexpectedly. Earnings may fall below expectations, for example.

More often, management decides to use working capital financing to grow the business more rapidly than annual cash flow can support. The customary bank lending arrangement is asset-based financing using the distributor's balance sheet as collateral. Specifically, banks lend up to certain percentage of the most liquid assets, receivables (75%-85%) and inventory (50%-65%). The advance rate percentages depend on various factors and some assets (seriously past-due receivables and dead inventory, for example) are not eligible collateral.

The strength of the distributor's balance sheet affects the bank's willingness to lend and the terms offered. Bankers prefer to lend to profitable distributors whose assets are not heavily leveraged. How much leverage is too much depends on the conditions. An old rule of thumb is that a conservative balance sheet has no more than $2 of debt for every $1 of equity (2:1 debt to equity ratio). The debt includes accounts payable to suppliers as well as bank loans. We see many distributors with debt to equity ratios far over the safe harbor ratio of 2:1. For more information on this subject see my *Official Guide to Distributor Finance.*[5]

The growth constraint must be evaluated before planning a major growth initiative. What is the shareholders' risk tolerance? What is management's risk tolerance? Managing a heavily leveraged distribution business is challenging.

Fast-growing privately owned distribution businesses often face a conflict between owners who want to invest in growth versus those who demand that the company distribute profits to non-working owners in the form of cash dividends or bonuses to owners who work in the business.

---

5 See my *Official Guide to Wholesaler-Distributor Financial Success.* Published by National Association of Wholesaler-Distributors, 2007.

Strategic planning projects are intended to uncover an array of growth opportunities. We expect the planning team to identify a series of choices that would require significant capital. Many distributors come out of the discovery process with a recommendation that the company take more advantage of leverage. One of the principles of strategic planning is that many companies don't have enough debt. The strategic profit model demonstrates how leverage magnifies return on investment.

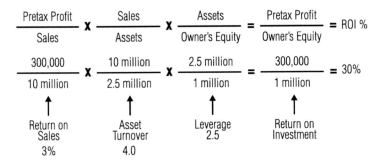

In the following example each change of only 0.5% in return on sales results in a 5-percentage-point change in return on investment. The dramatic multiplier effect for distributors is because of the high level of asset turnover and balance sheet leverage provided by no-cost supplier financing. For most distributors, 80% of assets are fast-turning receivables and inventory. In some trade lines suppliers finance 100% or more of inventory.

For this reason distribution truly is a game of inches where very small changes in margin or other factors have a powerful effect on return on investment (ROI). A distributor with only 2-3% pretax return on sales (ROS) can produce a strong pretax ROI of 20-30%.

In the era of historically low interest rates, a typical distributor experiences positive leverage because the return on assets of the business exceeds the interest rate paid on bank debt. For example, a business with a 2% return on sales and annual asset turnover of four earns a return on assets of 8% (2 x 4). Leverage is positive if the bank interest rate is less

Chapter 6 - The Compelling Goal & Growth Trajectory

than 8%. There are obvious risks to this approach. Distributor profitability is both cyclical and vulnerable to unpredictable ups and downs (losing customers, aggressive competitors, fickle suppliers, market swings, credit losses, to name a few). Interest rates change daily.

The bottom line is this: The rewards of growth may be enticing, but some people prefer to "eat well but also sleep well." Understand the financial realities of your business, and use them as a check on your growth plans before moving forward.

✓ STRATEGY CHECKPOINT

Use the following questions to gain a better understanding of the importance of creating and effectively communicating a compelling goal in your organization.

1. How do the people in your organization know where the company is going and how the leaders intend to get there?

2. If you have a stated goal, does it touch the employees in a meaningful way? How do you know?

3. Are the people in your company clear about the roles they play as individuals and team members in helping reach the stated goal?

4. How does your leadership maintain strong, two-way communications with people at all levels within your organization?

Chapter 7
Keeping Score: Three-Year Objectives & KPIs

Accounting is the language of business. As a recovering accountant, I'm always trying to find new ways to understand and share complex business ideas clearly and concisely. Devising ways to keep score works really well if everyone in the room speaks the same dialect; in this case the mother tongue is numbers.

Strategic planning for a distribution company is an exciting journey into an imagined future, not an accounting exercise. But as in baseball, a great scorekeeping system makes executing a strategic plan even better. As Peters and Waterman[1] said, who would want to go bowling or play golf if they couldn't see what happened and keep score?

Setting financial objectives for the next three years sets strategic planning apart from the annual planning process. While your Big Hairy Audacious Goal may take much longer than three years to achieve, the planning team must approach the process by asking themselves: "Where do we have to be in three years to be sure we're on the way to achieving our BHAG?" The choice of objectives for one, two and three years is in line with the three-year planning horizon and fits nicely with our primal urge to plan our businesses based on how long it takes the Earth to orbit the sun.

We urge distributors to change the way they customarily conduct their annual sales forecast and budgeting ritual. I'm not a fan of the top-down business plan starting with a sales forecast and predicting expens-

---

1 Tom Peters and Robert Waterman are authors of the popular management book *In Search of Excellence: Lessons from America's Best Run Companies.* Published by Grand Central Publishing, 1988.

es by guessing percentage increases over last year. (This is discussed more in Chapter 10: Mapping Out Your Business Plan.)

The annual business plan is more likely to take the company where you want it to go if the plan is tied into the three-year objectives, which are of course in tune with achieving your compelling goal. Each step of the way fits into a tracking system that follows a handful of critical measurements that tell you if something isn't going according to expectations. The measurements, or Key Performance Indicators (KPIs), are gears that move together toward the BHAG while making sure the enterprise is generating a return on investment sufficient to attract capital. The importance of the company's attractiveness to investors and lenders cannot be overstated.

Select a small number of powerful KPIs for strategic planning purposes. These KPIs will appear on your One-Page Plan. While there are many KPIs that are not financial – such measures of customer and employee satisfaction are often found in a "balanced scorecard" – this particular discussion is about financial measures only.

There are an almost unlimited number of financial KPIs for distributors to choose from, so I break them down into four types: return on sales, asset turnover, leverage and return on investment. Each is a component of the distributor strategic profit model discussed in Chapter 6:

$$\underbrace{\frac{\text{Pretax Profit}}{\text{Sales}}}_{\substack{\text{Return on}\\\text{Sales}\\3\%}} \times \underbrace{\frac{\text{Sales}}{\text{Assets}}}_{\substack{\text{Asset}\\\text{Turnover}\\4.0}} \times \underbrace{\frac{\text{Assets}}{\text{Owner's Equity}}}_{\substack{\text{Leverage}\\2.5}} = \underbrace{\frac{\text{Pretax Profit}}{\text{Owner's Equity}}}_{\substack{\text{Return on}\\\text{Investment}}} = \text{ROI \%}$$

$$\frac{300,000}{10 \text{ million}} \times \frac{10 \text{ million}}{2.5 \text{ million}} \times \frac{2.5 \text{ million}}{1 \text{ million}} = \frac{300,000}{1 \text{ million}} = 30\%$$

It's important to tie the financial objectives to the BHAG. For example, if the BHAG stipulates a future sales target, sales progress toward the growth trajectory connects the sales mileposts along the way to the goal. Variations might be to track order bookings, sales backlog of unshipped orders, new order entries, new customers, lost customers or percentage of quotations turned into orders. In another example, if the BHAG includes winning an award for being a great company to work for, the KPIs must include progress with the criteria for winning the award.

Return on Sales

This category includes KPIs that measure the effectiveness of managing business processes that result in a good (or bad) return on sales. The major subcategories are sales growth, margin, people expense and non-people expense. There are an almost unlimited number of minor subcategories under each. For example, for the sales growth major subcategory, KPIs could be new accounts opened, lost customers, sales calls, number of quotes, closing rate or sales cycle time.

Sales growth is at the heart of most distributor strategic plans and is frequently built into the BHAG itself. The growth trajectory is a long-term sales projection. Options for sales KPIs include total sales dollars, sales percent change versus a year ago, breakdown of sales into warehouse sales and direct shipments, or breaking sales into two or more major product groups or customer segments. Keep it simple on the One-Page Plan and drill down into components elsewhere.

Sales growth alone isn't meaningful without tracking margin percentage. It also goes by other names such as gross margin percentage, gross trading margin (GTM) percentage and gross profit percentage. Tracking could be simplified by combining the product of sales dollars times gross margin percentage into gross margin dollars. Options include breaking down gross margin percentage into components such as warehouse and direct shipment sales, product groups and customer segments. Again, keep it simple on the One-Page Plan.

The most consequential expense control measure is the personnel productivity ratio (PPR). PPR is simply total compensation including benefits divided by gross margin dollars. For example, if salaries, wages and commissions are $1 million and benefits total $250,000, total compensation equals $1,250,000. If gross margin dollars are $2,500,000, the company's PPR is 50%. Like golf scores, the lower the PPR the better. There is a strong positive correlation between low PPR and high profitability. We've seen some distributors with low PPR who weren't especially profitable for other reasons, but have yet to see a top-quartile performer (top 25% of industry companies based on ROI) who did not have a strong PPR.

Asset Turnover

In this category, major subcategories are cash, receivables and inventory.

Receivables and inventory are the two biggest distributor assets. Together they are usually at least 80% of total assets. Asset management is a primary driver of distributor return on assets (return on sales percent times asset turnover equals return on assets percent). Optimizing asset management is so critical that each of these assets deserves its own KPI on the distributor's one-page strategic plan. Inventory turnover is usually expressed with a measure indicating the average number of annualized inventory turns. There are nuances to the way this KPI is calculated but it is imperative that turnover include warehouse transactions only (no direct shipments), and that it is based on warehouse cost of goods sold, not sales dollars. If a distributor uses the LIFO inventory method for tax reasons, the KPI is calculated using FIFO inventory costing. For more on this, check out my *Official Guide to Distributor Financial Success.*[2]

 The most common KPI for receivables management is calendar days sales outstanding (DSO) based on trailing open account credit sales (not including cash sales and credit card sales). There are variations in

2 See my *Official Guide to Wholesaler-Distributor Financial Success.* Published by National Association of Wholesaler-Distributors, 2007.

Chapter 7 - Keeping Score: The 3-Year Objectives & KPIs

the method of calculation, however the most important consideration is consistency. Some distributors favor tracking percentage of past dues over 60 days beyond terms or 90 days beyond terms, but those measures can be distorted by heavy sales in a particular month. Tracking dollars outstanding alone doesn't measure management effectiveness as sales rise and fall from month to month.

Leverage

For the leverage category, the major subcategories are accounts payable, bank debt and possibly taxes. Think of the assets side of the balance sheet as a list of what the company owns and the other side (liabilities and equity) as a list of what the company owes. The total amount of the company's assets is equal to the total amount of the company's liabilities and assets. Every dollar of assets not financed by the owners' equity (original investment plus earnings retained in the business) is a debt owed to creditors.

Most distributors have two types of large creditors: suppliers and banks. Some distributors also borrow money from other lenders such as bondholders or shareholders. One of the critical elements of distributor profitability is the willingness of suppliers to help finance the business. Accounts payable to suppliers (assuming they are paid within terms) do not incur interest charges. As a rule, suppliers don't require collateral or guarantees nor do they impose loan covenants. In some trade lines supplier financing covers most or all of distributor inventory.

Bank financing comes at a price and may have significant strings attached. There is always a risk that the lender may decide to call a working capital loan or impose stringent limitations, especially if the distributor borrower has a drop-off in financial performance.

KPIs should include monitoring borrowing levels, especially if the business has bank loan covenants or is close to its maximum borrowing levels. In some cases a 13-week projection of cash flows is necessary. If so, KPIs should be designed to track the cash position versus expected cash needs.

Return on Investment

Finally, in this category, there is only one measurement: return on investment (ROI). In French the word "roi" means king. For investors, ROI is king.

 The key performance indicator for return on investment (ROI) is un-ambiguous: pretax income divided by equity equals ROI percentage. Use net income before tax so your result is comparable with other firms

Figure 7-1: Compounded Sales Growth Rate

The "magic of compounding" is a lesson that is sometimes underappreciated by investors and by business managers. As shown by the four growth curves on the chart, even a small change in annual growth rate compounds rapidly. A company growing sales at 3% annually would take 24 years to double in size; at 6% compounded growth sales would double in 12 years. Note that a rapid annual growth rate of 10% results in a doubling of sales in only 7 years.

Sales growth comes from a combination of three forces: rising prices, growth in the economy and increased market share. Some distributors seek to jumpstart their growth with a series of small acquisitions to add market share.

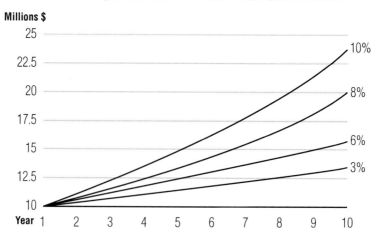

10-Year Compounded Sales Growth for $10,000,000 Distributor

(many nonpublic companies are pass-through entities that don't pay income tax) and to make year-to-year comparisons meaningful even when tax regulations and rates change. Net income for this measure is after all expenses except income tax. Interest expense is deducted from operating income to determine net income because it is the cost of borrowed capital used in the business. As mentioned elsewhere leverage is positive so long as the company's return on assets is greater than its interest rate on borrowed funds.

How much return on investment is enough depends on what rate is needed to attract capital to your distribution business. The magic number is what your investors and lenders expect. The lender question is the more straightforward of the two. Banks, the usual source of borrowing for distributors (other than suppliers), want to feel comfortable that they will be paid back in full and on time. If the balance sheet is fairly strong, the return on investment threshold required by bankers isn't as high as what investors expect. Bankers want to see enough cash flow to cover the agreed upon repayment of loan principal and interest, plus a small cushion of 10% to 20%.

Investor requirements are more fickle because their needs are different. Private equity funds and other financial investors may target 20% or more (pretax) compounded annual return. Keep in mind that the typical private equity fund hopes to sell off its investments within five to seven years of acquisition. This is a high return within a short time span.

Investors with more patient investment horizons expect returns consistent with perceived risk. Some distributors are large public companies but most of the thousands of wholesale distributors in the United States are fairly small. Investors in smaller firms expect a premium investment return because of the increased risk and lack of liquidity. Additional return is anticipated through appreciation in value if the company doesn't pay regular dividends.

A final note about inherent risk in wholesale distribution: The industry has low barriers of entry and exit that enable companies to come and go from local markets fairly easily. Distributors are dependent on the decisions of their major suppliers, and there is sometimes a significant amount of supplier concentration. We encourage investors in distributors to set a minimum pretax return on investment goal of 20%.

☑ STRATEGY CHECKPOINT

Answer these questions to drive discussion on how your company tracks progress on your goals.

1. How does your company set performance objectives each year? Does each year stand on its own, or do you link the annual periods to long-term goals for the business?

2. How does your management group track the performance objectives? How often does the team review results versus the plan and take corrective action?

3. Do you have a handful of objectives for the overall business and a subset of more detailed measures for each business unit? Do your managers set and track measures for the functional areas such as sales, operations, purchasing and credit?

4. What outside benchmarks do you use to compare your company's performance?

5. Does your company tie incentive compensation to your Key Performance Indicators?

Chapter 8

The Sweet Spot: Selecting Investments

By figuring out what to sell, whom to sell it to and where to do so, three basic distributor strategy riddles are solved. The harder part is deciding what very few important things need to be done exceedingly well to grow profitable sales within the targeted "sweet spot."

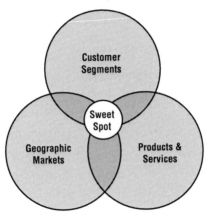

Not unlike making choices for a retirement fund, executives must select investments for their distribution businesses. If you fail to make the right commitments at the right time, you may miss opportunities or take unnecessary risks.

The big idea behind strategic planning is to invest where you see the best chances for meaningful, profitable growth. The following tools will help you do this.

Growth-Profitability Matrix

The first step is to clearly understand your current customer segments from the perspective of growth potential and profitability.

The growth-profitability matrix I propose for distributor strategic planning is an offshoot of a business model developed originally by Boston Consulting Group. The adaptation I make for distributors takes into account three vital pieces of information for each investment candidate:

- How much revenue do you have in this segment?
- How profitable is this segment?
- What do you see as the growth potential for this segment?

A bubble chart is the best way to depict three variables on a two-dimensional chart. The size of each bubble represents your company revenue in that segment. The bubbles are positioned along two axes, one of which is profitability in the segment and the other is assessment of the growth potential. In the example below, I have used gray, black and white to represent segments, but you can use different colors as a simple way to distinguish your sales to different customer segments.

Many distributors keep investing in their largest revenue segments, without regard to either growth potential or profitability, represented by the gray bubbles in the bottom left of the following chart. The black circles at the top right generate cash flow and merit additional investment. The striped bubbles at top left require some analysis to see if you

Figure 8-1: Growth-Profitability Matrix

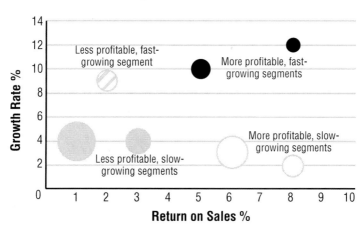

can make them more profitable with additional investment.

The lower right quadrant – the white circles – require the most careful review. You have validated that you can make money with these customers. If you invest in this segment – additional sales talent or technical expertise, for example – will it grow? This exercise allows you to see how best to adjust current resources to the areas with the best potential for return.

Segment Matrices

To get the most out of your strategic planning process, consider these three choices: Where will you operate; what products and services will you provide; and to which customer segments will you sell? Simply stated: what, where and to whom? At a time when markets are shifting, a review of these foundational questions will highlight where the biggest opportunities lie and help you focus.

Complete a Segment Matrix, as shown in Figure 8-2, for each of the three choices, or sandboxes: geographic markets, products and services, and customer segments. Each of the matrices has three possible choices for each decision – grow, maintain or harvest. Selecting grow means that this geographic market, product or service, or customer segment is targeted for investment of people resources and capital. The company

Figure 8-2 Customer Segment Matrix

Customer Segments	Grow	Maintain	Harvest
MRO	✓		
OEM		✓	
Contractors		✓	
Resale			✓
Government			✓
Healthcare	✓		

Chapter 8 - The Sweet Spot: Selecting Investments

 **CASE STUDY**

The Sweet Spot:
Home decor distributor targets adjacent markets
with right customer mix

A wholesaler of home decor products was the major supplier of its products but within a limited geography. Management said that it already had the customers it wanted in its market areas. Resources were limited, but the company felt that it could get the support of its major vendors and was determined to expand.

The planning team carefully evaluated what types of customers most highly valued the company's services and were most profitable to deal with. Research indicated which adjacent markets had the largest concentration of customers in the company's sweet spot. Further analysis identified the markets with the best logistics advantages and least direct competition.

As a result the company made a move into an adjacent market that had the right combination of customer mix, competitor weakness and vendor support. There was no ideal acquisition target so the distributor used a green-fielding approach.

will invest heavily to build its share of the market. Targeting must be done judiciously because all companies have limited resources of time and money. The strong temptation of distributors to target everything must be resisted.

The maintain choice is to keep the status quo. The company is determined to hold its position in this geographic market, for this product or service, or for this customer segment. Maintain means that the company will continue to invest enough time and resources to protect its share (percentage of the market).

Harvest means a distributor has decided to simply hold onto the customers it already has in this segment. It does not mean the distributor wants to lose the business it has in this area, but the company will not invest additional time and money trying to build its presence in that segment.

Geographic markets, products and services, and customer segments that do not figure into the company's future are not in the harvest category; they are to be left out of the segment matrix analysis altogether.

The three basic choices distributors make determine how the business deploys its people (especially sales representatives) and to some degree where it locates its assets (branch locations).

Geography

I like to start with geographic markets because it is the clearest set of choices. The geographic markets matrix requires a series of decisions about where the company will invest its capital for facilities and the market development efforts of its people.

Geographic expansion is the traditional form of distributor growth because it is easier than expanding into unfamiliar product lines and new vendors. The location where a distributor started is often thought of as the home market, a fortress where the company has historically been a strong player. As distributors grow they tend to move into markets close to the home market. Depending on the line of trade, expansion may follow as new branch locations, counter operations, retail stores or sales offices with a small amount of inventory. A series of acquisitions may result in additional "home markets" where the company has a very strong local presence.

Sometimes it makes the most sense to grow by moving into another area within your current markets. This logic applies to distributors who are reluctant to add a location in a new market, whether growing internally or by acquisition.

Certain suppliers play a powerful role in defining the expansion plans of their distributors. This is particularly true for distributors of exclusively or selectively distributed branded products, where the supplier awards authorization to distribute product lines within defined areas.

Planning Tip

The segment matrix is an exercise for small groups to work on and to report their recommendations to the planning group as a whole. The entire group can engage in a discussion that leads to decisions. I recommend that the teams assign this grow, maintain or harvest evaluation to each segment matrix item rather than checking two boxes or using pluses and minuses where the group has trouble reaching a conclusion.

The geographic market segment exercise may lead to a deadlock in which people want to grow every market. This problem can be resolved by carefully defining the categories. The growth category requires significant commitment of time and dollars to fully develop the company's market potential. The maintain designation indicates that the company intends to invest in a market where it feels its market share has reached its potential and a strong effort may be needed to protect market position. Even the harvest designation requires continued effort to protect existing customers even though the company does not intend to actively seek other customers in that market.

CASE STUDY

Finding the Right Mix:
Packaging distributor discovers unmet needs & transforms role in channel with services

Despite its efforts to diversify, sales at a large distributor of packaging supplies and equipment were concentrated in its North American automotive accounts. Management wanted to maintain its profitable volume in the automotive segment but felt threatened by widespread industry vendor consolidation and other cost-cutting initiatives. Other automotive industry threats included imported vehicles, "transplants" in the U.S. who preferred overseas suppliers and the nascent quality revolution.

The planning team carefully examined the current and emerging needs of its automotive customers and suppliers, and explored new services it could provide along with its packaging products, supplies and equipment. The team stipulated that it could do nothing to turn the tide at its customers. The distributor could only hope to anticipate change and to adapt faster and better than its competitors.

As a result the distributor found unmet needs including becoming an accredited quality certified supplier on behalf of its vendors, and providing quality control and inspection services as a qualified receiving facility for its suppliers. The distributor transformed its role in the channel from "time and space utility" to becoming an extension of both its suppliers' and customers' manufacturing.

The supplier may not be able to prevent shipment from an authorized location to customers outside the designated area; however, they are able to withhold sales and cost support as well as apply pressure in various ways.

The first step in the geographic market segment exercise is to decide which markets are included in the matrix versus being left off altogether. The next step is assignment of the grow, maintain or harvest analysis to each geographic market. The scope varies based on the size of the distributor. For example, a local company may look at new sales territories or small branches near its central location; a regional firm may consider opening (or closing) large branches in nearby geographic areas.

Products and Services

The products and services matrix is a series of investment decisions about deployment of sales resources and capital for inventory. The products and services matrix is complicated by the inclusion of both products and services in the same matrix. I suggest doing so because the products and services are usually woven together tightly. Traditionally distributors got into the services business out of necessity, the services being a means to the end of selling more product. The service demand may have come from customers or from suppliers, such as a requirement that authorized distributors perform warranty work or minor repairs on equipment. The decision to get into equipment may well have been an effort to sell more product.

Distributors often find making money on maintenance and repair work very difficult. The problem is made worse by inability to track labor and travel time and the cost of parts. Service technicians are often used to assist in sales presentations and provide other support.

The determination to grow a product line that requires services is also a decision to provide those services. Growth designation is a commitment to invest heavily in people and assets to achieve the company's full potential with a product line. Broadly speaking, it is feasible for distributors to develop services as a product center separate from product lines, but this is rare.

The decision to maintain a product line is a commitment to invest as needed to hold the company's market position or share of that product line. Doing so requires growing the business fast enough to expand with the market as well as to find pieces of business to replace those that are inevitably lost to competition or for other reasons.

Harvesting a product line is potentially difficult because of the way suppliers may react. The distributor's intention is to hold onto the customers already buying the products while not seeking other customers for those products. The resulting loss of buying power may be a problem even if the supplier is supportive. The decision to harvest a product line is sometimes a determination to replace the supplier's line with another line or to drop the unprofitable products altogether.

Some of the matrix decisions, as you can see, are based on knowledge of what's working and what isn't working for the distributor. The issue is where the distributor is making money and where the company is breaking even or possibly losing money.

It is much easier for salespeople to build sales with a product line they are familiar with and feel confident with than to be a market pioneer with a line they don't know much about. Some sources state that it is four times more difficult to introduce new product lines, even to a well-established customer, than to sell what the salesperson (and the company) is already proficient with. The decision to move into a totally new line is a difficult one because of the commitment of time and capital over a long period, possibly several years. This is a "zero sum game" when trying to sell a new line through the existing sales force. The new products will take sales time and energy away from established products. The new products must be more profitable, and have more growth potential, than those they will displace.

Many products have become more complex with the stunning growth of technology. Suppliers expect more technical expertise from their distributor sales forces partly due to a reduction of the size of some supplier sales teams. Customers often demand that distributors provide technical support for products and equipment including the ability to solve complex problems.

The technical evolution is both an opportunity and a threat for distributors in many lines. Some companies choose to solve the need for field technical support by adding technicians to the staff to assist the sales reps. Others are training their sales reps to provide more expertise. Adding new product lines may require hiring sales specialists for the new line, hiring more technically savvy sales reps or engaging technical support staff. The incremental costs place more demands on the profitability of the new line. The customers' current suppliers will react to the entrance of a new competitor to the field and a plan needs to be in place to deal with their responses.

Customers

The customer segments matrix has a great deal to do with sales force deployment. Whether or not sales staff specialize in certain segments, they get comfortable with the customers in the segments where they spend most of their time. Sales reps become more valuable to their customers when the reps are intimate not only with the customer's operation but also with the industry the customer is in.

The traditional distributor ways to segment customers, such as by Standard Industrial Classification (SIC) codes, are not necessarily useful for strategic planning. Instead consider segmenting customers based on what is important to them, how they buy and what it is needed to capture their business. Customer Profitability Analysis (CPA) and Cost to Serve (CTS) data and a "whale curve"[1] can be extremely valuable in segmenting customers.

---

1 See my book *In Search of the Perfect Customer.* Published by National Association of Wholesaler-Distributors, 2011.

Figure 8-3 Summary of Customer Types and Behaviors

	Auctioneers	Wheeler Dealers	Negotiators	Partners
Objective	Hottest Price	Low price & good service	Fair price and extra services	High ROI
Decision maker(s)	Junior buyer	Purchasing agent	Departmental managers	C-level executives
Selling cycle	30 days	6 months	6 months to 1 year	1 to 2 years
Access	Very easy	Easy	Difficult	Very difficult
Loyalty	None	Low	Medium	High
Question	What's your price?	Do you have it?	Where can I get it?	What do I need?
Seller	Grinder	Minder	Binder	Finder

Consider the following, first outlined in Chapter 5:

- **Auctioneers.** These customers buy from the vendor with the lowest price. A junior buyer has no loyalty to your company, and the selling cycle is 30 days or less.

- **Wheeler Dealers.** The decision-maker is a purchasing agent who wants low price, but also good service. The selling cycle is six months.

- **Negotiators.** This departmental manager wants a fair price and extra services. This customer will have some loyalty because the relationship is built on more than price.

- **Partners.** These customers are focused on value. The decision-maker is a C-level executive willing to pay a higher price if there is a return on that investment. The loyalty level is high, but it takes a long time to gain their trust, up to two years.

Segment your customers into these categories to help you better understand how you can better serve them.

The importance of looking at customer segments differently is tied to the sales function. The number and type of sales reps, and how they are deployed and managed are fundamental strategy questions for wholesale distributors. The customer segments matrix, as well as the geographic markets matrix and products and services matrix, drive the questions of: Which sales skill sets, and how many salespeople, do we need in this geographic market to sell these products and services to these customer segments? It makes an enormous difference if you are intending to grow, to maintain or to harvest. Like capital, sales power and technical capabilities are scarce resources. What's in short supply must be allocated with precision. It is a trap to say "grow" for every market, product, service and segment. The successful distribution business needs to focus people resources and assets on a small number of high potential (profitable sales) opportunities. The rest is maintained, harvested or dropped altogether.

For many distributors the driving force of their business is the deep knowledge of the customer and the customer's business. The old rule of thumb that it is four times harder to sell even a familiar product to a new customer than an established customer applies to new customer segments, as well. The decision to grow a new customer segment to its full potential for a distributor may require hiring new salespeople or specialists to focus on that particular segment. It takes significant time and effort to develop expertise, relationships and a good reputation in a new customer segment. Expect a reaction from entrenched competitors to your new sales and marketing efforts!

Most distributors operate in more than one geographic market. They may find different customer segment opportunities, and different product and service opportunities, in each market. They may encounter a different assortment of competitors (other distributors, suppliers selling direct, etc.) in the various markets. The distributor may be authorized for different product lines depending on the market.

By using this Segment Matrix, you can organize the variability in the way your markets are defined to make good decisions on resource allocation.

Bringing It All Together: Distributor Strategy Cube

We designed a distributor strategy cube to organize the three segment matrices – customer segments, geographic markets, products and services – into a three-dimensional object. Each face of the cube is a matrix for a specific geographic market. The two axes on each matrix are customer segments and products and services. The priority – grow, maintain and harvest – may be different on each face of the cube.

This distributor strategy cube is based on the premise that product lines

Figure 8-4 Distributor Strategy Cube

Each face of the cube depicts a different geographic market. If the distributor does business in six distinct markets, the cube would have six faces. The purpose of the cube is to illustrate that the combination of customer segments, product lines and services might be different in each geographic market.

Geographic Market B

	Product line A	Product line B	Product line C	Value-added services
OEM Customer	Grow	Grow	Harvest	Maintain
MRO Customer	Maintain	Maintain	Grow	Harvest
Contractor Customer	Harvest	Harvest	Harvest	Harvest
Govt Customer	Grow	Harvest	Maintain	Grow
Resale Customer	Harvest	Harvest	Grow	Harvest

Geographic Market C

Geographic Market A

and service offerings should be different in various geographic markets because customers and customer segments, and possibly product line authorization, vary from market to market.

Using the Strategy Cube:
PVF distributor picks different offerings
for different markets

A multi-location distributor of pumps and PVF operated in several distinct geographic markets. But management was not successful in its determined effort to sell the company's entire line in all markets. The product and support offerings were not tailored to the varying needs of customer groups in each market. The company did not have the support of its primary vendors in some markets, and also did not have proper technical support in all locations.

Using a strategy cube, with each face representing a different geography, the planning team agreed on a different, focused product and service mix for each market. The product mix was realigned to reflect the customer needs, vendor support and competition in each market. Management recognized that it did not have the resources to provide needed technical and sales support for every product in each market.

As a result the sales efforts were refocused on the best opportunities, and management and staff felt better about the company's reputation as "best supplier in the market" among its customers and suppliers.

✅ Strategy Checkpoint

Use these questions to get a start on drafting your strategy map by determining where best to dedicate your resources.

1. Which of your customer segments are most profitable, and have the greatest profit potential? Which ones must you defend to hold your share? Can you harvest any of them? Which customer segments you are not currently serving are attractive for development?

2. Which of your current geographic markets are ripest for profitable growth, which do you need to defend to maintain your position, and which can you afford to harvest? Which geographic markets you are not presently in offer the greatest profit potential?

3. Which of your current product lines are the best ones in which to grow, which must be defended, and which can you simply harvest? Which product lines you are not in now are the best ones to attack? Answer the same questions for services, as well as products.

4. How can you use the distributor strategy cube to diagram your markets?

Chapter 9

Breakthrough Initiatives

Some less seasoned participants in the strategic planning process may become impatient: "Enough about the past and the present. When are we going to talk about the future? Let's do something!" The debate about initiatives is what everyone has been waiting for.

The discussion that will lead to breakthrough initiatives should start with the general and move toward the specific. Talking about themes is a good way to set the stage for this part of the planning.

Scenarios enable team members to visualize and interpret what the business may look like moving forward – people, customers, products, services and so on. The size of the business is a prime factor in determining the right strategy. If the company is smaller than most of the competitors that matter it may need to get bigger to thrive in the future. Another option for the smaller company that wants to stay small is to specialize, to find and fill a profitable niche. The specialty has to be big enough, important to customers and something that the company can be the best at providing. Getting bigger, or specialized, is moving forward. Doing nothing is standing still, a choice that may ultimately make it necessary to get out of the business – sell or liquidate, or do something else entirely. The team needs to internalize why standing still is dangerous.

A strategic breakthrough is an action that will move the company toward its BHAG in line with its growth trajectory and three-year objectives as expressed by the KPIs. Leadership has a big challenge in coming up with breakthrough initiatives: You need to settle on two or at most three. Every company has a finite amount of people resources and capital. Every business competes on speed.

Winnow the long list of candidates toward the two or three breakthrough initiatives that best meet the company's success criteria: big enough to make a difference, realistic, executable and practical enough to complete in the time available.

The planning team has already made the grow, maintain and harvest decisions in the three categories: geographic markets, products and services, and customer segments. Think of these three sandboxes as "what" we need to do. The breakthrough initiatives are "how" we can get this done. Here are five areas to discuss when determining initiatives.

Customer Intimacy

The sales function is central to customer intimacy. I refer to the sales function as the profit engine that finds customers and binds them to the company. The architecture of the sales function may be outside sales reps calling on customers, proactive inside sales reps, reactive customer service reps, technical support reps, sales specialists, electronic commerce, direct mail marketing, or some combination of these methods. The structure for delivery of technical support may be technically proficient sales reps, technical field support specialists, phone support, web-based support or some combination. The staff structure, however it is designed, can be deployed in many ways: by geographic territory, by customer industry, by customer size or complexity, by product group, and so on. Study the distributor W.W. Grainger for ideas about stratifying the customer base and designing different models for intimacy with each type of customer. Sales organization structure and deployment is a strategic decision for distributors.

Operational Excellence

There are also many choices for achieving operational excellence. I stated earlier that the discipline of customer intimacy equals operational excellence. The inseparability of the two disciplines doesn't mean that the customer dictates how the distributor responds to customer needs – that is a strategic decision for the distributor. Consider the fastener distributor who locates a warehouse next to each of the company's largest customers and stocks every item the customer uses, or the retail supplies distributor who locates a warehouse next to the regional distribution center of the company's largest retailer accounts. Think about the medical supplies distributor who positions employees inside the company's hospital customers to deliver supplies within the facility. Building an information system to provide seamless multichannel marketing for pricing information and placing orders is strategic. Building a nationwide network of third-party logistics providers linked to the information system is strategic. Optimizing inventory turnover and fill rates, for example, are tactical.

Supplier Intimacy

I want to introduce the notion of supplier intimacy for wholesale distributors. Supplier intimacy for distributors is key to supply chain excellence. The philosophy of working with an elite group of suppliers as "partners" is strategic. The suppliers and distributors are not "partners" in the legal sense but rather as parties to a joint venture. The objective of the joint venture is to win customers who depend on the distributor for the supplier's products. Think of the supply chain relationship between Procter & Gamble and Walmart, between McDonald's restaurants and its dedicated distributors, or between the grocery and foodservice distributor McLane Company and its customers. Beating up suppliers for discounts and rebates is tactical.

Another supply chain and merchandising decision with strategic implications is brands. Supplier intimacy suggests that commitment to supporting a supplier's brand is critical but this is not always true. Many outstanding suppliers are delighted to manufacture private label products. Some major distributors have had notable success with development of their own brands. Other distributors have done well with "white box" (no registered brand name) products. Consider a truck parts distributor who is the major player selling brand-name products

Figure 9-1: Distributor Strategy Themes and Options

Strategic Themes	Explanation
Keep on keepin' on	Some distributors resist change as they seek to "eat well and sleep well" by sticking to what they know best and avoiding risk.
Acquisitive distributor	The serial acquirer wants to jumpstart growth by buying competitors rather than building the business themselves.
Vertical integrator	Distributors sometimes want to move "upstream" by forming strategic alliances with manufacturers and converters. Others go "downstream" by getting into services such as kitting, assembling, packaging, repairs and maintenance.
Innovator	Distributors may focus their efforts on helping customers solve difficult problems. Solving old problems in new ways requires a high level of customer intimacy as well as technical expertise.
Branding expert	Some distributors have done very well designing products and developing their own brands.
Good, better, best	Distributors following this theme offer distinct levels of products and services to meet varying needs of different accounts rather than "one size fits all."
Marco Polo	The "customers in search of products" theme applies to distributors who specialize in carrying hard to find items, or in searching out special products for their customers.
Product experts	Product-focused distributors have warehouses full of products in search of customers. They know their product applications well and seek to push product into the marketplace.
Distributor as consultant	Distributors acting as true consultants have solutions in search of problems. They have proven expertise learned from working with customers and are available for hire.

in a large, well-established market. When the company tried to bring this model to a new market, it failed due to wide customer acceptance of white box products, especially low-cost imports. The company re-launched the branch's strategy with white boxes and their own distinctive service program and is doing very well.

Firm Design

Wholesale distribution organizations have alternatives for design of the firm. At the root level, the company management may be centralized or decentralized to varying degrees. Large companies have become more dependent on information systems and telecommunications systems to manage the businesses. The systems have facilitated centralization of many functions such as financial reporting, information systems, human resources and credit management. The idea of centralization can be very appealing to executives who aspire to achieve control over the company without duplication of expense and unnecessary travel. The quest to centralize can overlook the fact that customer intimacy and operational excellence take place "on the ground" and close to the customer. Customer-facing activities are often best executed at the local level.

The temptation to centralize all seven of the functions (sales, operations, purchasing, accounting, information systems, credit and human resources) can be self-defeating. Marketing is a department in large distributors. Even at smaller companies the various marketing tasks such as negotiating deals with large suppliers and designing marketing programs can be done centrally, however we find that merchandising and reordering is best done closer to the customer. Vendor mix, customer preferences and competition vary from market to market.

Regarding branch management, some distributors designate the sales manager as the top person at a smaller branch (i.e., a branch not large enough to have a general manager). Other distributors place the operations manager in charge of such a location. Another variation is to have the branch sales and operations managers report to senior managers outside the branch with no one individual in charge of the branch itself. The overall organization structure has strategic implications, however I feel the way small branches are managed should depend on the talents of the people available and is a tactical decision.

Wholesale distributors must be organized around the needs of their customers. Certain functions can be centralized, such as financial reporting, credit management, human resources and information systems. For

Planning Tip

Creative thinking – the words imaginative, resourceful, original, inventive, ingenious may come to mind – is a process. Experts have devised systems that help business teams become more creative. I have been trained on Carl Robinson's "Six Hats of Critical Thinking " where team members take turns wearing six different color baseball caps or T-shirts, each color signifying an attitude (white = positive, black = negative, green = creative, etc.) during the discussion of a proposal.

My point is not that baseball caps are needed, but rather that each one of the planning team members is capable of being creative in the right situation. Research shows that people like to think of themselves as being creative. We need to take full advantage of that: a small planning team of subject matter experts, well prepared, well rested and in ideal surroundings. Finally, the team leader and facilitator must create the optimal atmosphere: non-threatening, not judgmental, relaxed but with the right degree of focus.

Your idea of the best environment for creative thinking may be serene: a quiet room with comfortable places to sit or stretch out, or possibly an isolated cabin in a forest or in the mountains. Our experience is that getting away from the company offices is necessary. It is also critical to disconnect the planning team from the distractions of its information and telecommunications umbilical cord. Create the optimal conditions for creativity. A cozy cabin isn't that important, but quiet, pleasant surroundings and reasonable isolation from the company for a few hours is.

most distributors the sales and operations functions that touch customers must be managed close to the customer. The physical presence of the purchasing function is debatable. Inventory replenishment is a local matter whereas marketing (deal making with major vendors and pricing) can be a centralized function.

Regardless of your perspective on the value of centralization versus decentralization, no two companies are exactly alike. Distribution markets are highly fragmented. This final step is important to make sure your strategic planning analysis is tailored to your company's unique set of attributes and circumstances.

Leading and Management

Companies have different approaches toward leading and managing people. Some businesses establish policies and procedures and hold their people accountable, while other firms have much less structure and train their people to use good judgment and "do the right thing." Another dichotomy is the range of distributors who use open book management at one extreme and other firms who are highly secretive at the other extreme. I have preferences about these cultural questions, but I don't have the data to support an opinion about these choices being strategic success factors. When it comes to company culture so much depends on company traditions and the character and charisma of the leader.

There is, however, one leadership decision that does seem to have strategic implications. Think of leaders who treat their employees as highly valuable (non-balance sheet) assets, assets worthy of continued investment and ongoing maintenance. Compare those leaders with ones who behave as though their employees are an operating cost on the income statement, an operating cost that must be kept at a minimum. Our findings over many years of working with distributors, and examining the data from all sources, indicates that distributors with a smaller number of more highly compensated people do much better than firms with a larger number of lower-paid staff. As a benefit of lower turnover, distributors with more experienced staff have fewer errors, lower training costs and greater customer satisfaction (as evidenced by customer retention).

Initiatives

The next step in the strategic planning process is breaking the planning group into small teams to evaluate a series of ideas for initiatives (thought-starters) proposed by the facilitator based on the planning process to date. Each small team is responsible for dropping thought-starters from the list, modifying the remaining ones and coming up with totally new ones. Each idea is a seed for what may become a proposal for an initiative. The small teams take turns pitching their ideas to the group. The group kicks them around, combining similar ideas from the other teams, modifying, rejecting and adding new ideas. The planning team can take the surviving ideas from the first round and cycle them through the small teams again or act as a committee of the whole from that point on.

The winnowing process is a vetting of each idea against criteria such as these:

- Is the idea big enough to make a difference? Will it "move the needle"?
- Is the idea realistic?
- Can the company afford to finance it?
- Is the company's staff capable of executing the idea?
- Is the idea practical enough to complete in the time available?
- Is the idea manageable?
- Can results be measured and monitored for corrective action?

The outcome of the vetting exercise is a 'yes or no' decision on each idea. The surviving ideas are candidates to become strategic initiatives. The planning team needs to conduct a beauty contest by comparing

CASE STUDY

Taking Action:
Material handling equipment distributor diversifies customer base, product offering

A supplier of material handling equipment was heavily dependent on two very large but cyclical customers. The sales leader wanted to diversify the customer base to include smaller customers whose needs could be met with off-the-shelf products. But the engineering leader insisted that selling low-cost standardized products would dilute the company's hard-won reputation for its design-and-build capabilities.

The planning team obtained research showing that the market for highly customized equipment was too narrow. By "confronting the facts," the team broadened the company's product line to appeal to customers for high-quality, low-cost standard products with fewer features. Structured brainstorming sessions, based on market data, were held with the company's board, engineers and sales team.

The data helped break down the barriers between engineering goals and customer needs. As a result the company diversified its customer base and product offering to include quality equipment that could be sold to smaller accounts at an acceptable profit. When the capital equipment market recovered the company was able to capture an even greater share of customized product orders.

each initiative with the others. A business case can be made for each initiative. The business case is a mini business plan detailing the staff and resources needed, a timetable, Gantt chart, budget, and so on. The business case must include an assessment of the risks involved, as well as the potential success.

A word of warning: There is an inherent danger in an assessment activity involving business cases. Details in a business case invite criticism of new ideas. Be careful that promising initiatives aren't screened out by "the loudest voice in the room" or thinking such as "we tried that once and it didn't work." The naysayers will have their opportunity to shoot down ideas. Nailing down the two or three best strategic initiatives is an exercise in the art of leadership and change management.

A good process for comparing candidates is ranking them based on criteria such as capital and people needed, time and effort required, projected influence on reaching your compelling goal and likelihood of success. The rankings inform discussions of what needs to be done to make your compelling goal happen.

✓ STRATEGY CHECKPOINT

Here are some questions to help you be more productive when you deliberate breakthrough initiatives.

1. What is your company's track record for execution of strategic initiatives? If you don't feel good about it, what are the root causes of poor execution? Most management teams try to do too much. Can your team agree that it would be preferable to successfully attack two or three winning moves?

2. What is your team's usual process for making critical decisions? Does it work? How could the leadership improve the outcomes? What role could an outside facilitator play?

3. Is the leadership group clear about the difference between winning moves versus merely fixing things that are broken?

Chapter 10

Mapping Out Your Business Plan

General George S. Patton knew much about wartime planning and execution, and many of his aphorisms are memorable ("Lead me, follow me or get out of my way.") and applicable to business situations ("A good plan violently executed now is better than the perfect plan next week.")

To paraphrase Patton: There are three ways that business leaders get what they want: by planning, by working and by praying. Any great business takes careful planning or thinking. Then you must have well-trained people to carry it out: That's working. But between the plan and the operation there is always an unknown. That unknown spells defeat or victory, success or failure.[1]

How can you get what you want from your distribution business? Your strategic plan is only the foundation. By itself the strategic plan can't be accomplished. The management team must map out the details for carrying out the plan.

Your company already has an annual planning process backed up by quarterly, monthly, weekly and daily plans and meetings. Achieving your compelling goal requires harnessing the energy of your organization through your business management processes. Those processes may need to be tweaked, reinforced or even redesigned. Executing the strategy should not be a new activity or project for the company; it is built into the way the business is managed.

---

1 As quoted in "The True Story of The Patton Prayer" by James H. O'Neill in *Review of the News* on Oct. 6, 1971.

The strategic plan needs to be connected to the annual plan for each of the years within the plan's three-year cycle. Think of them as Year One, Year Two and Year Three. The one-page strategic plan includes Key Performance Indicators (KPIs), which are checkpoints about where the company needs to be as it moves through the three-year period. Financial objectives describe where the company needs to be at the end of Year Three to be moving toward the compelling goal.

Why Top-Down Doesn't Work

The annual planning ritual at most distributors is a top-down undertaking, the premise of which is the relationship between three numbers: projected revenue, estimated gross margin percentage and expense budget. The three numbers are not well-correlated (that is, they're inconsistent with one another). The data is fed into a computer that forms a sausage called the annual plan. Add a little spice to adjust and out

Figure 10-1: Plan Linkage

The arrow moving from left to right shows the connection between the strategic plan, as expressed through the compelling goal, financial objectives and strategic initiatives, and the daily to-do lists on the far right. The current strategic plan is the basis of each year's annual business plan (as opposed to simply looking at last year's results and tweaking here and there). The annual plan is carried out through quarterly actions, monthly and weekly meetings, and daily activities. The items on each person's daily list should be directly connected to executing the strategic plan and to the annual business plan.

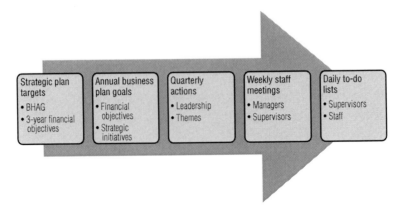

Strategic plan targets	Annual business plan goals	Quarterly actions	Weekly staff meetings	Daily to-do lists
• BHAG • 3-year financial objectives	• Financial objectives • Strategic initiatives	• Leadership • Themes	• Managers • Supervisors	• Supervisors • Staff

comes a plan complete with a projected net income.

Typical distributor annual planning is troubling for several reasons. Consider the following dreary but realistic annual planning scenario for a hypothetical distributor:

The sales forecast comes from the field and is wildly optimistic. Sales managers cajole their sales reps into projecting sales increases that can only be described as best-case. In turn the regional managers badger the sales managers to inflate the revenue numbers further due to bulldozing from senior executives and the CEO. A notable exception to the optimism rule is the possibility that the sales organization has financial incentives based on exceeding the forecast, in which case the numbers are "sandbagged." This situation only increases the arm-twisting from upper management who suspects the foul play.

The expense budget arises from the functional managers and is greatly exaggerated. The managers seek to avoid being beaten up during the year for not meeting budget. They also desire authorization to add staff in their departments and to budget good raises for people, both of which make managing easier and tend to increase compensation for the manager doing the budgeting. The CFO goes through the line items with a fine-tooth comb and haggles with the managers, anticipating bludgeoning from senior executives and the CEO.

The reality of these unpleasant activities is a net income projection that is a synthesis of inefficient and unreliable methods. The projected net income and capital expenditures plan are used for critical cash flow forecasting. Mistakes result in inadequate borrowing capacity (i.e., running out of cash) and the potential breach of lending covenants.

I advocate a bottom-up annual planning process that starts with the most important objective on the one-page strategic plan: return on investment (ROI). How much return is needed to attract capital (equity and borrowed funds) to the business? The demands of the owners and lenders, including suppliers, must be met if the company is to have a future. Net income for next year is simply revenue minus cost of goods sold (gross margin dollars) less expenses.

Here's what you should consider when doing the math:

Revenue

Revenue expectations must be tempered against three marketplace realities:

What economic growth is expected?

The economic growth question is not purely macroeconomic, in the sense of the entire economy or even regional economic expansion or contraction. The specific concern is the micro-economy, the customer segments in the region and particularly major customers. Have customers announced hiring or layoffs, plant openings or closings? How will expected acquisitions or divestitures help or hurt volume?

What price changes are anticipated?

Similarly, the subject of price changes is not in the context of the overall economy. The concern is with what is known or expected about major suppliers' pricing intentions and an informed opinion about when the changes will occur and the likelihood of acceptance in the market.

What share of competitors' business are we positioned to capture?

Finally, management must grapple with the challenge of gaining market share both by capturing customers from competitors, as well as increasing penetration at established accounts. Data from the field about targeted business and contracts already gained and lost is useful. Naturally competitors are planning to attack and include business they want in their plans for the coming year. Who will win more of those battles? Which companies are best positioned to grab a bigger slice of the overall market and more of the best customers' wallets? Management must confront the reality of how well their company is positioned in each geographic market, for each customer segment and with its products and services. Does the company have enough talented salespeople on the street? Are they highly qualified? Does the company have the right product lines? Does the business block and tackle well (high fill rate, timely delivery, low error rate)?

Margin Expectations

Judgment must be applied to lofty margin expectations, as well. The company's ability to increase margins depends on some of the variables mentioned in the preceding paragraph (sales talent, product lines, blocking and tackling). Pricing success relies also on the company's pricing architecture and processes: how prices are set, how much autonomy the sales force has, availability of market pricing data, how the sales reps are managed and incentivized. We have seen too many firms automatically plug a 50- or 100-basis-point (0.5% or 1%) margin increase into the plan each year, often for no apparent reason.

Expense Budgeting

Expense budgeting is just another forecasting exercise. The quick-and-dirty approach for budgeting non-people expenses is to simply assign a percentage increase to last year's expense amount on each line item. It is just as hasty to slash or even cross out expense lines without researching what the benefits of the expenditures are and how customers are affected. Each expense line must start over each year from zero with a buildup of dollars allotted to each expenditure based on how the investment affects customers.

People expenses are more sensitive and complex. Each functional area must list each individual and the annual cost of his ongoing employment: hourly including overtime, salaries, commissions, bonuses, fringe benefits, etc. The budget for the coming year must include a provision for compensation changes, bonuses, overtime work and changes in fringe benefit programs. The effect of timing of compensation changes is too large to overlook.

After the first pass, the bottom-up approach calls for iterations to the expense budget to produce the required net income based on the expected gross margin dollars. Subsequent versions of the expense budget force management to make difficult choices and trade-offs about people and non-people expenses.

Three Sets of Annual Business Plans

The assumptions behind any forecast and budget are fluid. But the assumptions are critical because of the cascading effect on the resulting sales and margin forecasts and naturally on the expense budget. It would be hasty to slash expenses prematurely based on a draconian forecast that turns out to be wrong. I suggest three sets of annual business plans: base case, worst case and best case.

Management should feel somewhat more than a 50% confidence level in the projected sales and gross margin projections and other assumptions underlying the base-case plan. Let's use a 60% confidence level.

The base-case plan outlines the people and non-people expense budgets needed to produce the required amount of net income, along with a capital expenditures budget and cash flow forecast. The base-case plan is used for meetings with lenders and for tracking business performance against plan.

The worst-case plan is based on a scenario that management feels is the most negative sales and gross margin that can reasonably be anticipated, essentially a situation in which many of the assumptions behind the base case plan turn out badly. Management should feel that the maximum chance of the worst case happening is 20%. The worst-case plan reveals the expense budgets needed to produce the required net income under the most disappointing conditions realistically expected. This contingency plan implies diligent tracking of actual results against the base plan. Management must act quickly if warning signals are detected during the year. The effectiveness of the backup plan is negated when there is too little time available to take meaningful steps.

Figure 10-2: Bottom-up Distributor Expense Budget

The bottom-up expense budget illustrates two important principles. First, each of the three cases assumes that the distributor must generate $1 million of cash flow. That may be the amount needed to avoid breaching a loan covenant. And capital expenditures of $50,000 are required to preserve the viability of the business. Second, each of the three cases or scenarios depicts the gross margin dollars resulting from different sales levels. The controllable expenses are changed in each case to meet the $1 million cash flow requirement. Management feels that there is at least a 60% chance of achieving the base-case sales level and not more than a 20% likelihood of the worst-case scenario.

	Base Case	Worst Case	Best Case
Sales	20,000,000	15,000,000	25,000,000
Cost of goods sold	16,000,000	12,000,000	20,000,000
Gross margin $	4,000,000	3,000,000	5,000,000
Gross margin %	20%	20%	20%
Required cash flow	1,000,000	1,000,000	1,000,000
Interest expense	250,000	300,000	200,000
Depreciation	300,000	300,000	300,000
Capital expenditures	50,000	50,000	50,000
Operating expense budget	3,500,000	2,550,000	4,450,000
Non-controllable expenses	1,500,000	1,500,000	1,500,000
Controllable expenses	2,000,000	1,050,000	2,950,000

The best-case plan is the mirror-image of the worst case: a scenario that management feels is the best sales and gross margin result than can be rationally anticipated, again with a maximum likelihood of 20%. Ironically, unexpected rapid growth can create a cash flow crunch for distributors. The cash box is quickly drained when the dollars are needed to buy inventory and carry receivables, not to mention sudden capacity expansion.

The one-page strategic plan includes other KPIs that are built into the annual plans such as expense ratios (personnel productivity) and asset management (receivables and inventory).

Driving the breakthrough initiatives through the annual plans for Year

One, Year Two and Year Three requires staging the initiatives for action at the appropriate times. Implementation depends not only on happening sequentially but also when the organization can afford (people and capital) to move ahead.

The breakthrough initiatives are broken down into a series of implementation steps. Use a Gantt chart for this purpose. For some initiatives the steps can be expressed as quarterly themes during Year One, Year Two and Year Three. In turn a series of monthly programs can tie into and support the theme for a particular quarter.

Figure 10-3: Gantt Chart for a Distributor Strategic Planning Project

Henry Gantt was an American engineer who devised the popular project planning tool that bears his name in the early 1900s. Applied to a strategic planning project, the sample Gantt chart depicts 12 major project steps to be completed over an 11-week period. An important feature of the Gantt chart is assignment of each task to an owner or owners. Another key feature is the clear indication of which tasks must be completed before another is started, and other tasks that can be undertaken simultaneously.

Step	Tasks	Who	Wk 1	Wk 2	Wk 3	Wk 4	Wk 5	Wk 6	Wk 7	Wk 8	Wk 9	Wk 10	Wk 11	Future
1	Detailed analysis of the company	Evergreen												
2	Private interviews with planning team members	Both												
3	In-depth survey of entire staff	Evergreen	X	X										
4	Research industry, suppliers, markets, competitors	Evergreen	X	X	X	X	X	X	X					
5	Panning team meeting day one	Both		X	X	X								
6	Planning team meeting day two	Both			X	X								
7	Draft one-page strategic plan	Evergreen					X							
8	Planning team conference calls	Both						X	X					
9	Finalize one-page plan and narrative	Evergreen						X	X					
10	Implementation team conference calls	Evergreen								X				
11	Implementation plan and Key Indicators	Evergreen									X	X		
12	Implementation team conference calls	Both											X	X

Answer these questions to get a good gauge on how you can better link your business plans to your strategic plan.

1. Has your management team been guilty of delaying needed actions while waiting too long for more information or for a better idea? What is your management philosophy about taking the risk of acting too soon versus the dangers of waiting too long? How does the leadership react to General Patton's viewpoint?

2. Does your business usually make the numbers in the annual plan? Why or why not? Do the people in the company take the planning process, and the plan itself, seriously? Does incentive compensation depend at least in part on achieving the expected results? How could the annual planning process be improved?

3. Is the business plan connected to the company's strategic plan? What are the assumptions that form the basis of the business plan based on? How are they validated?

4. What management techniques do you use to bring life to the business plan? How are the various elements of the plan communicated to those who need to know? Does the business use quarterly themes at the company, branch or department level to drive the results? Are results versus plan, and corrective actions, discussed at monthly and weekly staff meetings?

Chapter 11
Monitoring & Execution

We have worked with many distributors who suffer from a leadership problem I can describe only as Executive Attention Deficit Disorder. It manifests itself in many forms but the root cause seems to be similar: The leader is willing to try almost anything to make the business better. The vice presidents and the managers say things like, "The CEO brings fresh ideas back from her YPO Forum (or Vistage group, or seminar or trade show) and pushes us in yet another direction." The new push may contradict projects that are already underway, and the business goes in circles like a ship without a rudder. Managers learn to live with the indecision and lack of direction, saying, "This too will pass. The CEO will forget all about the new idea before long."

We are concerned about the ability to execute when management has a long list of projects that have been started and not completed, or not started at all. It's not uncommon for items on the list to be from two to three years ago or more. Many items on the to-do list are obsolete or shouldn't have been on the list to begin with. We also find two crucial types of items on these lists: repairs needed for major gaps and strategic issues. Part of the due diligence when getting ready to work on a strategic planning project is to revisit plans from the past. Sadly the track record we see on execution of past plans is terrible.

The roles of the people in executing the strategic plan vary. Once the strategic planning process is complete the members of the planning team return to their "day jobs." Disbanding the planning team is symbolic because it signals that the team members are responsible for their own roles in achieving a Big Hairy Audacious Goal. Breaking up the team also makes it clear that monitoring results and making adjustments is built into the organization and its operating units. There is no "eye in the sky" looking after the plan's outcomes.

The time to execute your strategic plan is limited. If you wait, your biggest risk may be losing the most profitable customers to competitors.

First, focus on closing the gaps that need to be fixed for the breakthroughs to work. The precious time needed to fix gaps delays execu-

Figure 11-1: Distributor Sales KPI Card

Key Performance Indicators (KPIs) must be changed periodically in response to changing business conditions and company goals. This example is for the sales function in a distribution business. The KPIs measure results for profit drivers such as order size and margin percentage; financial levers such as customer inventory and receivables; account development and even pricing realization. The measures in this case are Trailing 12 Month (TTM) numbers with a green/yellow/red indicator to show if progress is on track.

	Formula	TTM*	TTM YR AGO	G/Y/R
Gross Margin %	all sales	26.2%	24.8%	Green
Average Whse Order Size	whse sales/orders	$440	$390	Green
Operating Profit/Order	per CPA report	$14.50	$13.90	Green
Special Stock	$ investment	$131K	$92K	Red
Receivables DSO	trailing 3 mos	44.2	39.3	Red
Account Penetration	% (estimated)	67%	61%	Green
Customer Retention	lost accounts	9	6	Green
New Accounts	new accounts	15	9	Green
Pricing Realization	% potential	94.1%	92.2%	Green
Pipeline	$ in pipeline	$140K	$150K	Yellow

*Trailing 12 months

tion, but it is necessary to get business fundamentals in good working order.

Next, consider your communications plan. A distributor's commitment to strong, two-way communications ensures everyone understands the company's compelling goal, that each individual understands his role in achieving the goal, and that trust will be built and maintained through ongoing effective conversation. A good communications plan makes the successful execution of your strategic plan much more likely.

Staff meetings are a primary strategic planning communications medium. Plan monitoring and analysis must be on the monthly or biweekly staff meeting agenda using a Key Performance Indicators report. The meeting chair must direct the group to drill down into each KPI that is lagging for root causes and corrective action. (See Figure 11-1.)

Everyone in the company needs to understand the importance of looking into the future as far as possible. You don't want the organization to misinterpret long-term thinking and business planning as being comparable to the staggering Soviet Union's fabled five-year plans. Employees must expect that like a ship on a long voyage, the company's course will be adjusted according to sea conditions and weather, but the destination will not change. The staff needs to be educated so that adjustments won't be misinterpreted as failure. Even failure itself, should it happen, is a learning experience that can propel the company forward. It is also evidence that the company is bold enough to experiment with new ideas, that the organization is resilient and has the courage to continue to explore other opportunities to grow and prosper.

Track Your Progress

I recommend using a "green-yellow-red" monthly report to track progress on breakthrough initiatives. The report gives visual indication of the status of each assignment on the Gantt chart.

- Green indicates the task is on-time and on-target.

- Yellow indicates the task is behind-schedule or below-target but is expected to return to green status within one to two months.
- Red indicates the task is in trouble.

The group must jump on any task that is in trouble to decide what is to be done: Modify the task, provide assistance or possibly reassign the task. A task that is in yellow status on more than two consecutive reports is considered to be in trouble.

Task	Who	Jan	Feb	Mar
Task One	Albert	Green	Green	Yellow
Task Two	Connie	Green	Yellow	Green
Task Three	Chuck	Red	Yellow	Green
Task Four	Roger	Green	Green	Green
Task Five	Tracy	Yellow	Yellow	Red

If a company's strategic plan is to succeed, if the compelling goal will be achieved, every task no matter how small must end up on the right person's daily task list at the right time – whether the CEO or employees deep in the organization chart – and that person must complete that task before checking it off his list.

CASE STUDY

Talking Back:
HVAC distributor makes communication a priority through annual and quarterly meetings

An example of an excellent communications program is one that was designed by a large regional plumbing and HVAC distributor. The company arranges an annual meeting of all employees at a high school auditorium centrally located to its 20+ branch locations. Two meetings on consecutive weekends are needed to accommodate more than 500 people.

The CEO and other leaders spend a half day updating the entire company about accomplishments and challenges, presenting awards and celebrating excellence and talking openly about what the company needs to do during the coming year and beyond. The CEO also presents a 45-minute monthly webcast to all employees with current events, recognition and updates on the company's progress.

The company's 80 executives, managers and supervisors meet four times annually for communication and leadership training, as well as an annual two-day training event. There are also regular executive committee meetings and an annual retreat for the top 15 leaders.

✅ STRATEGY CHECKPOINT

These questions will help you determine how the culture in your company will contribute to or challenge your ability to successfully monitor and execute your strategic plan. Understanding your current state will help you understand what steps need to be taken to improve accountability at your company.

1. What is the culture of accountability at your company? How do you decide who will be in charge of a project? Do you hold one person responsible for success or failure of a project, or spread (dilute) accountability over a group of people? What could you do to improve the chances of success?

2. Do you commit to parity of authority and responsibility whereby the person (or group) responsible for execution is given the authority and resources they need to get the job done?

3. How does your management team track results for complex, critical projects? Do you use special meetings and reports, or do you incorporate project monitoring into the regular staff meetings?

4. How quickly does the management team jump in to help when a project isn't going well? Does the group let the project leader sink or swim? How rapidly does management act when it becomes apparent that the project needs to be radically changed or even scrapped?

5. Does your team tend to rely on complex, highly detailed reports or simplified and straightforward exception reports?

Chapter 12

A Culture of Planning

These days, with a 24-hour news cycle and the ability to track everything in real time, we are nearly always focused on the Now. For business owners the current crisis is always front and center. The latest recession exacerbated that tendency.

In today's global economy, it is critical to shift from a short-term survival focus to long-term growth mode. Strategic planning is a key differentiator for distributors, and it's more important than ever to understand your markets clearly. Strategic planning is about gaining that understanding, and then making decisions to create the best pathways forward, even in turbulent economic times. Knowing where you want the business to go will ensure you have the right resources and employee skill sets to get you there.

The steps outlined in this book are only the beginning. The next step is to inculcate your organization with a culture of planning and, more importantly, execution.

I've said this before and I'll say it again: Planning is where too many distributors stop. While more distributors are creating strategic plans now than 30 years ago, there are still frightfully few who have formalized the process. And many have not made the transition to executing the plans they create. They leave the planning process full of excitement, but they're not good at driving the plan through the organization. For a plan to be executed, it has to be on your day-to-day to-do list.

Another element of this I'll leave you with: Whether you are running a division in a large company or you are the owner-manager of a small distribution company, succession planning is the natural next step in strategic planning. Succession planning is about preparing for the inevitable departure of the owners or managers, and having the right pieces in place when that happens. Along with ensuring a clear road map after you leave, the strategic plan should involve key managers in making decisions that affect the company in both the near- and long-term. A strategic plan helps make the transition as seamless as possible for the next generation of owners and managers.

Good luck!

About the Author

Brent R. Grover founded Evergreen Consulting in 2001 as a boutique firm to advise companies in the wholesale distribution channel. He had been CEO and co-owner of National Paper & Packaging Co. Brent is also an Adjunct Professor at Case Weatherhead School of Management. Before his distribution industry career he was with Arthur Andersen & Co. Brent won the Elijah Watt Sells Medal and Ohio honors for his performance on the Uniform CPA Examination. Brent is a member of several non-profit boards and is Past Chairman of the National Paper Trade Association. He currently serves as a board member of B.W. Rogers Co., Famous Enterprises, Snavely Forest Products and Elkay Plastics.

Brent can be reached at brent@evergreen-consulting.com.

Visit Evergreen Consulting at www.evergreenconsultingllc.com.

About the Publisher

Gale Media publishes business information, research, software and market analytic tools that help wholesale distribution companies and their business partners run better. It is the publisher of Modern Distribution Management, a newsletter for wholesale distribution professionals since 1967, as well as mdm.com, a website that reaches an audience of more than 20,000 wholesale distribution executives with industry news and analysis, webcasts, books and other educational materials.

Gale Media is also the parent company of Industrial Market Information, a markets research firm that provides market size and end-user segmentation analytics and software for industrial product marketers in the U.S., Canada and Mexico. IMI's market analytics clients include more than one-third of the top 20 industrial distribution companies in North America. More information is available at imidata.com.